Dear Grandma

I wanted to send you
a Personalized note because
of how much it means to me
that you bring the family
together.

As you will read, Community
was key to the development of the
Chicago Innovation Ecosystem, and I
value the Community of our family.

With much love,

Avery

RISING
TOGETHER

The Story of Chicago's Innovation Ecosystem

By ★CHICAGO INNOVATION

Additional Books by the Authors

Co-authored by Thomas D. Kuczmarski and Luke Tanen

Innovating...Chicago Style: How Local Innovators are Building the National Economy

Co-authored by Thomas D. Kuczmarski and Dr. Susan Smith Kuczmarski

Apples Are Square: Thinking Differently About Leadership

Lifting People Up: The Power of Recognition

Values-Based Leadership

Also by Thomas D. Kuczmarski

Innovating the Corporation

Innovation: Leadership Strategies for the Competitive Edge

Managing New Products: Using the MAP™ System to Accelerate Growth

RISING
TOGETHER

The Story of Chicago's Innovation Ecosystem

By ⭑CHICAGO
INNOVATION

⌐BOOK ENDS
PUBLISHING

Cataloging information available from the Library of Congress.

Publisher: Book Ends Publishing, Chicago, IL 60614

Editor: Jacob Sherman

Cover design: Rui Weidt, Tanen Directed Advertising

Page design: Rui Weidt & Linda Kornmeyer,
Tanen Directed Advertising

Printed in the United States of America.

This book is dedicated to the Chicago Innovation sponsors, board, staff, community collaborators, and members, without whom there would be no authors of this book, and to the Chicago Innovation Award past winners and nominees, without whom there would be no story to tell.

TABLE OF CONTENTS

ABOUT THE AUTHORS

Rising Together: The Story of Chicago's Innovation Ecosystem is a collaborative effort written by members of the Chicago Innovation team, leveraging insights from the thirty-one individuals interviewed.

Now in its nineteenth year, **Chicago Innovation** empowers the Chicago innovation ecosystem by educating, connecting and celebrating innovators. The organization's vision is to solidify the Chicago region as a global leader in innovation and ensure that innovation is for everyone. Its flagship program, the Chicago Innovation Awards, recognizes the most innovative new products and services brought to market each year in the region. Additionally, Chicago Innovation hosts monthly events, and is home to three region-wide programs: the Chicago Student Invention Convention, the Women Mentoring Co-op and Ageless Innovators, an intergenerational co-mentoring program.

Thomas D. Kuczmarski is the President and Founder of the global consulting firm Kuczmarski Innovation, and an internationally recognized expert in the innovation of new products and services. He is also the co-founder of Chicago Innovation. Tom is a longtime professor at Northwestern University's Kellogg School of Management and has published eight books on innovation and leadership. He is the chairman of the Chicago Innovation Board, a trustee on the Retirement Research Foundation Board, a board member of the Chicago Inventors Organization, and a member of the Economic Club of Chicago, Executives' Club of Chicago, and Commercial Club of Chicago.

Luke Tanen is the Executive Director of Chicago Innovation. Focused on driving growth at the organization, he oversees the recruitment of sponsors and fundraising activities, provides counsel on events and programs, and manages the Chicago Innovation Awards nomination process. Luke's first co-authored book, *Innovating...Chicago-Style: How Local Innovators Are Building the National Economy,* profiles some of Chicago's most innovative companies. Luke received his undergraduate degree from Northwestern University and his MBA from Northwestern

University's Kellogg School of Management. He is a member of the Economic Club of Chicago, Executives' Club of Chicago and was previously selected to *Crain's* "20 in their 20s" list in 2014, which annually recognizes twenty young leaders who are on the rise.

Paul Kitti is the Events Director for Chicago Innovation, where he oversees the planning and execution of the Chicago Innovation event series, which attracts over seven thousand attendees annually and includes the production of the largest annual celebration of innovation in the Midwest – the Chicago Innovation Awards. Paul was previously in the startup trenches at Red Frog Events, where he was involved in the conceptualization and execution of national brands including Warrior Dash and Firefly Music Festival. Previously, Paul worked as an entertainment journalist in Ann Arbor and Detroit. He received his undergraduate degree from the University of Michigan.

Jacob Sherman is the Head of Public Relations and External Affairs for Chicago Innovation, as well as a Senior Associate for Kuczmarski Innovation. He is responsible for sharing the stories of Chicago's innovators and their impact on the region, and introducing new people and organizations to the Chicago innovation ecosystem. In his time at Kuczmarski Innovation, Jacob has worked with B2B and B2C clients in various industries resulting in multiple tested portfolios of new offerings valued at over $400M in cumulative three-year revenues. Jacob is also the Editor for Book Ends Publishing, where he has worked on the award-winning *Lifting People Up: The Power of Recognition (2018).* He has been featured on WGN Radio's *Opening Bell*, and sits on the Board of Directors for The London Idea. Jacob received his undergraduate degree from the University of Wisconsin-Madison.

Avery Stone Fish is the Program Manager for Ageless Innovators, Chicago's first intergenerational co-mentoring program and community built intentionally to value diversity of perspective, and Program Manager for the Corporate Startup Matchmaking program. Avery is also a Senior Associate at Kuczmarski Innovation, where he trains executives on how to develop portfolios of new-to-the-world products, services, and business models. He serves on the Bridging Generations Board for The Village Chicago, the

Associates Board for JCFS, and the Young Professionals Board for P33. Avery also performs regularly at Second City, and has written, produced, and performed music across the country. Before joining Chicago Innovation, Avery received his undergraduate degree at Northwestern University, where he was the mascot.

ACKNOWLEDGMENTS

To the innovators and industry leaders who donated their time and shared their personal reflections, histories, opinions, and recommendations to guide the creation of this book, we thank them. This story could not be told without the help of the thirty-one individuals we interviewed. These include: Brian Bannon, Brenna Berman, Hardik Bhatt, Holly Copeland, Linda Darragh, John Flavin, Mike Gamson, Chris Gladwin, Sandee Kastrul, Michael Krauss, Amanda Lannert, Ross Manire, Matt McCall, Dan Miller, Caralynn Nowinski Collens, Hedy Ratner, Harper Reed, Taylor Rhodes, Kristi Ross, Mike Rothman, Terry Savage, Jai Shekhawat, Marc Shiffman, Howard Tullman, Shivani Vora, Ed Wehmer, David Weinstein, Kevin Willer, Maria Wynne, Sam Yagan, Andrea Zopp.

To Dan Miller, Co-founder of Chicago Innovation, for believing in and sharing the stories of Chicago's innovators before anyone else would, we thank him.

To Mitch Hufnagel, we thank him for his help during research efforts.

To Rahm Emanuel, Lori Lightfoot, J.B. Pritzker, and Toni Preckwinkle, who have supported Chicago Innovation, validated our efforts, and shared a greater vision for the future of the city, we thank them.

To the countless members, leaders, founders, and connectors of the Chicago innovation ecosystem not mentioned in this book whose stories could fill volumes longer than a single binding could ever hold, we thank and applaud them.

INTRODUCTION

by Thomas D. Kuczmarski

A little over twenty years ago, in December 1999, many of us were scared that we would soon be locked in elevators and our computers would crash; Y2K was around the corner. The level of chaos expected was enormous, as people feared that computers would be unable to operate when the date rolled over from "99" to "OO," and the two-digit dates would switch back to the beginning of time. But, in the end, we all survived.

During that same time, when the consequences of shifting technology were a looming concern, Chicago was just beginning to see the emergence of a community focused on innovation and entrepreneurship. Few realized it back then, since large corporations were still the face of the business world with corporate CEOs playing the role of business hero. But deep underground, the seeds had been planted. Startups would continue to sprout and grow over the next two decades to become a major force driving economic growth for the region.

Back in 2002, we started the Chicago Innovation Awards to recognize and celebrate innovators of all types in Chicago. This inclusive mindset surrounding innovation was key, and led to the essential ingredient for success: recognizing innovators from big corporations, startups, nonprofits, academia, and government all under one roof. This meant different kinds of innovation too, both incremental and disruptive, as well as high-tech, low-tech, and no-tech.

For years, I have defined innovation as creating and capturing new value for customers, consumers, constituents, or end-users that an organization serves. There was so much value creation and capture occurring in Chicago in the early 2000s, but few people knew about it. So, I wanted to shine a spotlight on all of the amazing innovations that were bubbling up across industries during that time. Over the past eighteen years, we have seen entrepreneurs continue to flourish, start-ups surge, incubators explode, and the innovation landscape evolve into a supportive and capital-ready culture. But while an incredible amount of progress has been made, the city is rarely viewed or recognized at large as a center for innovation.

That is why we decided to write this book.

Rising Together tells the story of how the business community of Chicago has transformed from a large corporate town into a hub of innovation that today supports and cultivates innovators, entrepreneurs, inventors, and leaders who think differently about growth, problem solving, and collaboration. It is about regional impact that occurs when individuals, organizations, values, and goals all come together to guide a communal culture – Chicago style.

At the center of this innovative and entrepreneurial ecosystem is the powerful value of collaboration. This spirit of working together and giving back has been an essential component to Chicago's success. We have come a long way during the past twenty years, and we believe this story should be shared. There are still, of course, several issues that must be addressed in order to sustain the future growth of the city. Crime needs to be drastically reduced, public education must continue to be enhanced, and we need to connect all of the neighborhoods of Chicago to become a single, livable, and safe community. We need to become an even more inclusive city, and open doors for people to advance, connect, and excel.

We decided that although we have been listening to and sharing the stories of Chicago's innovators for many years, we could not tell this story alone. On the following page is a list of the thirty-one Chicagoans that we interviewed for this book. They are leaders that cut across the public and private sectors, across industries, and represent many of the people who have been instrumental to and supportive of the evolution of the Chicago innovation ecosystem over the past several years. The growth of the ecosystem is largely a result of the actions taken and initiatives spearheaded by these people. In addition to them, there are undoubtedly hundreds of other key people that have been equally as constructive to this cause, and to all of them we give a huge thank you and nod of appreciation.

This book should fill Chicagoans with pride, for the journey we have taken over the years has not been an easy one. And for people outside of Chicago, who may be searching for ways to create a community of innovators of their own, welcome to the story that has shaped Chicago into a connective and transformative place to innovate.

INTERVIEWEES

1. Brian Bannon — Director, New York Public Library; Former Commissioner & CEO, Chicago Public Library

2. Brenna Berman — CEO, City Tech Collaborative; Former CIO, City of Chicago - Department of Innovation & Technology

3. Hardik Bhatt — Leader, Digital Government, Amazon Web Services; Former CIO, State of Illinois

4. Holly Copeland — Senior Director of Corporate Social Responsibility, Sustainability & Impact, Horizon; Former Deputy Director, Office of Entrepreneurship, Innovation, & Technology for the State of Illinois

5. Linda Darragh — Executive Director, Northwestern University's Kellogg School of Management Innovation & Entrepreneurship Initiative

6. John Flavin — CFO, Endotronix, Inc.; Former Head of the Polsky Center for Entrepreneurship and Innovation at the University of Chicago

7. Mike Gamson — CEO, Relativity; Former SVP, Global Solutions, LinkedIn

8. Chris Gladwin — CEO & Co-founder, Ocient; Founder & Former CEO, Cleversafe

9. Sandee Kastrul — President & Co-founder, i.c.stars

10. Michael Krauss — Co-founder, Market Strategy Group

11. Amanda Lannert — CEO, Jellyvision

12. Ross Manire — Former President & CEO, ExteNet Systems

13. Matt McCall — Partner, Pritzker Group Venture Capital

14. Dan Miller — Co-founder, Chicago Innovation; Former Editor, *Crain's Chicago Business*; Former Business Editor, *Chicago Sun-Times*

15. Caralynn Nowinski Collens — CEO, Dimension Inx; Former CEO, MxD (formerly UI LABS)

16. Hedy Ratner — Founder & President Emerita, Women's Business Development Center

17. Harper Reed — Former CTO, Obama for America; Former Head of Commerce, Braintree; Former CTO, Threadless

18. Taylor Rhodes — CEO, Applied Systems; Former CEO, SMS Assist

19. Kristi Ross — Co-CEO & President, tastytrade

20. Mike Rothman — Founder & Chairman of the Board, SMS Assist; Co-founder, Theron Technology Solutions

21. Terry Savage — Nationally-syndicated finance expert and author

22. Jai Shekhawat — Founder & Former CEO, Fieldglass

23. Marc Shiffman — President & CEO, SMS Assist

24. Howard Tullman — General Manager, G2T3V; Former Executive Director, Kaplan Institute at IIT; Former CEO, 1871

25. Shivani Vora — Managing Director, Accenture Innovation Hub

26. Ed Wehmer — President & CEO, Wintrust

27. David Weinstein — Founder & CEO, Freshwater Advisors; Former Founding President, Chicagoland Entrepreneurial Center

28. Kevin Willer — Partner, Chicago Ventures; Former Founding CEO, 1871; Co-founder, Google Chicago Office

29. Maria Wynne — CEO, Leadership Greater Chicago

30. Sam Yagan — CEO, ShopRunner; Former CEO, Match Group

31. Andrea Zopp — President & CEO, World Business Chicago; Former Deputy Mayor of Chicago and Chief Neighborhood Development Officer; Former President & CEO, Chicago Urban League

CHAPTER

1

A CITY OF
INNOVATION

CHAPTER 1: A CITY OF INNOVATION

The Building Blocks of a Community

On a Saturday morning at the corner of S. State St. and E. 33rd St., seventh graders Aanya Sahu and Florian Halimi load their ChargeAir power generator into Aanya's mom's car. They just found out they'll be headed to the National Invention Convention, where their homemade portable wind turbine will eventually take home the country's Visioneer Award. For now, they're thrilled to have completed the four-month innovation process leading up to the Chicago Student Invention Convention. National awards, patents, and early investment rounds haven't yet entered their minds. But they soon will.

Twenty-five miles west, in the suburban flatlands, the multi-billion-dollar hidden giant, Molex is working on its own automotive innovation. Founded eighty years ago as a flowerpot manufacturer, it's now planting the seeds for the future of transportation. The innovators at Molex are building an Ethernet network solution for autonomous vehicles, an intricate system of sensors and connectors that constructs the nervous system of a smart car. Radical innovation in corporations, though less common than in startups, is nothing new. Molex is relentlessly innovative, as if their thirty-six thousand employees depend on it. And they do; in today's climate, a company's race for impact and survival runs on the same fuel.

Innovation also fills the tanks of a burgeoning class of startups across the Chicago region. One such example is NuCurrent, a leading developer of high-efficiency antennas for wireless power applications. The idea behind the company started with a group of students at Northwestern University looking to develop medical technology to ease spinal pain. Their problem was: how does one recharge a device implanted in the human body? This question led them to develop a wireless power antenna, and the company pivoted to bring this technology into consumer products.

NuCurrent emerged thanks to an ideal environment for successful startup innovation: a fertile ground fit for identifying problems, sharing ideas, and collaborating; an ability to move quickly on new ideas; the flexibility and openness to allow an idea to evolve into previously unseen solutions; and, access to resources that spur scale.

These are individual stories of innovation, but this story is much bigger. It's a *city's* story of innovation. Chicago is much like other future-forward cities in the race to deliver products and services capable of solidifying themselves as global leaders. But what makes the sum greater than its parts, and what makes the city itself poised to evolve into its own innovation-generating machine, is how individual stories like these are connected.

A Formula Emerges

A kids invention program. A large corporate innovator. A successful tech startup. These entities exist in other cities, but their connection in Chicago is special.

NuCurrent was born from Northwestern University's Farley Center for Entrepreneurship and Innovation, a program designed to identify, foster, and fast-track entrepreneurial initiatives from its student participants. Now increasingly common in top universities, this kind of program was a rare find back in 2009. Fast-forward a few years into their startup, and the group is selected to participate in the Illinois Science and Technology Coalition's "Corporate-Startup Challenge."

An initiative propelled by state government programming and sustained by a combination of community and city-government support, the Corporate-Startup Challenge sought to connect budding startups with progressive corporations wise enough to see the value in partnering with small emerging businesses. Here, Molex met NuCurrent, and it was love at first sight. NuCurrent's patented design and inherent agility combined with Molex's worldwide distribution and manufacturing capability formed something more powerful than either could achieve on their own.

Returning to Aanya, Florian, and their ChargeAir, where do they get their platform to innovate and compete? On the same stage where the team would eventually receive their ribbons and recognition at the citywide convention, just eight feet above their heads flies the Molex logo as a sponsor of the Chicago Student Invention Convention. Is Molex paying it forward, investing in the future of their community? Most definitely. Are they also nurturing a line of potential future investments? It's not crazy to think that a company founded in 1938 might have a long-term strategic plan with tethers to the community.

Collaboration and support combined with connection making and recognition. A university program birthing a startup identified by a government competition and connected with a corporation that is funding a student innovation program that is inspiring tomorrow's innovators. A formula emerges.

These connections are what power the innovation ecosystem.

The Word of the Day

The symbiotic chain of events detailed here is just one of an infinite number of potential outputs from an innovation ecosystem that is mature enough to spurn economic growth. There is a blueprint for the city of the future, and when followed, it can turn a city of disparate innovators into a city with a long-term, self-sustaining innovation ecosystem.

But before diving in deep into how all of this happened, it's important to understand the crux of the ecosystem. What is **innovation**? Take a second, close your eyes, and define it for yourself. We'll wait.

For many, rather than a single, concise definition of innovation, a word cloud comes to mind. Nouns like creativity, invention, risk, technology, and entrepreneurship make frequent appearances. Or verbs like ideate, problem-solve, and change. All of these play into innovation, and many companies today pride themselves on being "innovative."

Getting on the same page about what innovation is (and why it's important) is key to understanding the blueprint for an innovation ecosystem. In this case, the best way to define innovation might be by describing what an innovator does. An innovator identifies a real problem or need. One that hasn't yet been solved, or is ripe for a more efficient solution. An innovator then addresses this need in a way that is unique; perhaps she creates a totally new solution, or instead takes something that already exists but has never before been applied to this particular need. An innovator then sees the new value that has been created from her solution, and it isn't long before there is an observable impact in the marketplace.

In short, innovation refers to the process of identifying a need, and then developing a unique solution that creates and captures new value in a way that significantly impacts the market.

An innovation ecosystem is an environment that not only supports innovation, but makes innovation inevitable. An innovation ecosystem is complex in its makeup and internal processes, but simple in its mission: drive regional economic growth. It doesn't take an urban planner or economics major to understand that all societies exist within some form of ecosystem where the success or failure of one piece can influence outcomes for others. Many in the U.S. saw this concept laid bare during a particular event not too long ago: Amazon's public search for the location of their second headquarters.

When Cities Self Reflect

In 2018, Amazon's very public hunt for a new city to call partial-home spurred what essentially became the Great Beauty Pageant of American Cities. Perhaps it was clever (maybe even innovative) of Amazon to turn the table and demand their potential suitors put their best foot forward; or maybe it was ultimately a publicity-driven dog and pony show that left some cities catching their breath and wondering why they expended so much time, money, and hope.

One clear positive from the endeavor, however, was that it did nudge established powerhouse cities and sleeper potentials alike to engage in some serious self-examination. Yes, the pageant contestants were excited to be courting the dashing Amazon, but they were more excited about the tangential opportunities that such a trophy partner could provide over time. Could bringing home this behemoth tech-center spur long-term job growth? Could it attract more talent to their backyard? Could it lift them into the national conversation and expose some of their long-standing strengths? Perhaps it could inspire investments into improved urban transportation, a revitalized downtown, an influx of new students to their local universities, or the emergence of a trendy district inviting new restaurants, breweries, and small businesses.

The notion that a sudden implantation of a giant puzzle piece can make an entire ecosystem complete upon impact is perhaps wishful thinking. Depending on the initial condition of the region, the puzzle piece may never find the right grooves to settle into, or might get rejected outright as unfit. There is no "quick fix" innovation ecosystem. It has to be built intentionally over time, and needs to be values-driven at its core.

The concept of cities as complicated cultural ecosystems is not entirely new. But cities entering the conversation as serious *innovation* ecosystems have higher goals in mind than, for example, where they stand on the most-populated city list. Size still matters in an increasingly globalized economy, but not like it used to. Other factors include job creation at a rate that matches consistent population growth, the implementation of sustainable practices to ensure a safe environment, and many other variables that play into the traditional idea of a healthy city on a good trajectory.

Through properly leveraging innovation at scale, the opportunities for any city to become a major player in the global economy are more accessible than ever. As competition for attracting citizens with a passion to advance humanity increases, a new standard for a city's ecosystem emerges. Innovation has been proven over the past several decades as a key economic stimulant, and a citywide ecosystem is the model.

Breadth and Depth

Today's cities need to view themselves as diverse ecosystems built for innovation. Leaning too heavily into one industry can be devastating in the long-term. While hard-earned designations like "Motor City" and "Silicon Valley" quickly bring to mind industry dominances (past and present), they also come with a risk. A city with an economy built around one industry may have difficulty developing an integrated and self-promoting community, because an innovation ecosystem is cross functional, inclusive, and collaborative in its very nature. It has breadth; a word that will pepper the conversations around Chicago's uniqueness.

Breadth and diversity are vital for a healthy ecosystem, including breadth across industries, sectors, institutions, company sizes, diversity of employees, and especially in the types of products and services that are developed and brought to market. Thinking broadly about who plays a role in the ecosystem, it is crucial that innovation is for everyone: for students, for entrepreneurs, for corporate leaders, for people of all backgrounds and passions, for technologists, for artists, for academics, and for non-profit leaders.

Innovation isn't limited to a single industry, and neither is an ecosystem. Any industry can be flipped on its head in a matter of months because of the emergence of a new player disrupting norms and changing business models. In the wake of the tech boom, the value and potential impact of startups has grown more than ever before. Beyond their ability to quickly corral expert teams and develop new products and services that send waves of disruption across the marketplace, they play a key role in incentivizing their competitors to meet the ever-advancing status quo.

An Ecosystem Affords Access

One essential function of an innovation ecosystem is to create an environment where ideas can turn into businesses that create jobs, make movement in the marketplace, turn investors' focus onto the region, and provide opportunities for others in the community. Startups are often the first manifestation of these groundbreaking ideas, and are a frequent and important piece of the puzzle. However, it's important to note that a true innovation ecosystem isn't solely designed to churn out startups; it's designed to cradle ideas of any origin that may have the potential to make the ecosystem stronger as a whole.

There's an understanding among all stakeholders that whatever is fed into the ecosystem will eventually pay back dividends in the long run; a notion that helping people in the surrounding region is a part of a long-term strategy for making everyone stronger. This is why an innovation ecosystem can be measured by the closeness of its community, advanced by collaboration, and validated through celebration.

Intrinsic within this attribute of connectedness is access. New ideas need access to blossom; they need clear pathways of access to investors, accelerators, showcases, or partners. An innovation ecosystem is built to facilitate access.

Taking a final look back on Aanya and Florian's ChargeAir prototype, it is evident how several "access" opportunities helped this idea along. And there will be more to come if and when these young inventors decide to take advantage of them. They were fortunate to ideate within an ecosystem that was made up of systems that encouraged innovation. Beginning with the community leaders who developed the invention program, the teacher who adopted it into her curriculum, and the parents who took time after work to take Aanya and Florian to hardware stores so they could transform their idea into something tangible, the first steps to success began with a set of shared values favoring problem solving and idea generation.

As the concept moves from dream to reality, larger players like Molex make growth possible for those without resources by funding the invention program. As the young inventors choose whether or not they wish to evolve into entrepreneurs, they will need to seek access to more funding, more education, and more like-minded people who can join in building their idea into a business.

Perhaps they will plug into a university accelerator like NuCurrent did, or benefit from a government-funded program designed to fuse connections between local startups and corporations. There are an unfathomable number of Aanyas and Florians around the world. Are they encountering the same level of encouragement and resources to build their ideas? Do they have the luxury of looking around and seeing inspiration and role models whose paths they can follow? Are they being celebrated for their inventiveness, but impeded by a lack of resources to turn ideas into action?

The next wave of innovators and entrepreneurs will face intense obstacles in the pursuit of creating their new businesses, much like those that came before them. However, as regions recognize the value of developing a culture in which innovation is nurtured, initiatives are put into place to systematically lower these barriers to entry.

Chicago's innovation ecosystem is a banner example of how a widespread, values-driven culture has the power to drive economic growth. For those hoping to create a similar culture within their own circles, Chicago might serve as a model for how it can be done. It is no easy task to establish this type of cultural ecosystem, and it takes more than a few tech unicorns or government initiatives. In this case, the story of how Midwestern values, a balance of capital, and several individuals playing outsized roles came together to create a culture of innovation and entrepreneurship takes place over the course of a generation.

CHAPTER

2

CREATING AN INNOVATION ECOSYSTEM

CHAPTER 2: CREATING AN INNOVATION ECOSYSTEM

Chicago as Innovators

"We have to connect the dots; it will be the key to our future success," Microsoft's former Citizenship Director Shelley Stern often said over the past twenty years. "We have so many organizations in Chicago that are doing great work to advance innovation, entrepreneurship, and technology." But the question is, how does a region leverage all of these disparate components in a way that expands the innovation pie and creates an ecosystem in which innovation truly is for everyone?

Large corporations are no longer the sole breadwinners in the race for job creation, and as more and more entrepreneurs find success through startups, the attention has shifted from trees to forest in terms of how innovation can act as a regional cornerstone for growth. By taking a look at the grand-scale effectiveness of an innovation ecosystem, people have uncovered a better approach to fostering a tech and entrepreneurial community that contributes to the overall growth of a city or region.

Since 2002, the year that the Chicago Innovation Awards was founded to celebrate the most innovative new products, services, and businesses in the Chicago region, there has been an unprecedented uptick in the growth of new startups, alliances, partnerships, incubators, and corporate innovation occurring in Chicago. A new business is created just about every day, and those businesses are growing fast. According to Pitchbook and the National Venture Capital Association, Chicago companies raised a decade-high $2.186 billion in 2019, which funded 279 different organizations across the city.

Chicago's startups aren't just breaking the bank, they're also breaking new ground. The city has the highest concentration of female startup founders than any other city in the U.S.; according to *Inc. Magazine*, nearly 34 percent of the roughly three thousand startups today are run by women. Chicago continues to be ranked first in new and expanding corporate locations in the country, and has been ranked number one in direct foreign investment in

North America for the seventh consecutive year as of 2019. The city is home to the top-ranked business school (University of Chicago's Booth School of Business) and business incubator (1871) in the world. Rising through the ranks to become a top ten global innovation hub as recognized by KPMG, Chicago is a far cry from the industrial town it once was in the 1990s.

Howard Tullman

General Manager, G2T3V

Former Executive Director, Kaplan Institute at IIT

Former CEO, 1871

Best day of my career:

"One of my websites is in the Smithsonian. I was awarded a Presidential medal when that happened in 1993. That was a big day, a seminal kind of thing."

Fun Fact:

By age ten, Tullman had built a candy business and a magic performance business, foreshadowing his future as one of the city's most prolific serial entrepreneurs.

The Big Company Town

In the 1990s, the "tech entrepreneur" finally burst onto the scene as more and more people were learning about the capabilities of the Internet. Linux, Microsoft, Java, and others, led to the development of dotcom companies left and right that were deviating from the traditional corporate path and building technology-centered businesses of their own.

But these groundbreakers were few and far between, and by the early 2000s, a number of people and organizations in Chicago were seeing more of a need to connect and foster a community of these innovators. As Jai Shekhawat, Founder of Fieldglass, recalls, "In the early Internet days, a lot of dotcom ideas were silly – not really innovation. Back then, real innovation was done at large corporations. We're talking innovation with a big 'I.' The smaller firms were not having much luck." Chicago in the 1990s was still a large corporation town, and the mindset for many back then was that entrepreneurs were rather unimportant to the economy.

With large corporate innovators running the show in industries like pharma, technology, and healthcare, there was little desire or incentive to work collaboratively with other organizations. Chris Gladwin, Founder of Cleversafe and Ocient, remembers a time when the big innovators lived effectively on islands of their own: "U.S. Robotics was awesome and dominated a huge market, but it was pretty isolated. And Motorola was an even bigger success in its time, but also stayed fairly secluded. Their whole model was creating lifetime employees."

At the time, the innovation landscape had been mostly comprised of large corporations, often located in the suburbs, built up tall with moats around their corporate headquarters to keep people from coming in and out. Matt McCall, Partner at Pritzker Group Venture Capital, remembers, "During the nineties, it was a 'big company' town. Success was a corner office, and a big one at that." Howard Tullman, a serial Chicago entrepreneur, recalls, "We didn't have a lot of startups. It was like pigeons fighting for breadcrumbs."

It was a difficult life for the early entrepreneurs, and as Howard described, it was a competitive and unpredictable experience. Linda Darragh, now a professor at Northwestern's Kellogg School of Management, recounts some of her early ups and downs as an entrepreneur: "Divine Interventures was founded in 1999, but crashed hard a few years later. By 2001, things were still going up and down."

Linda wasn't the only one who faced a difficult transition from the nineties into a new millennium. Even those that were looking to supply the entrepreneurial community with talent faced some woes. In 1998, Sandee Kastrul founded i.c.stars with the goal of becoming the source of talent for the many dotcoms that were popping up left and right. Says Sandee, "Everyone was preparing for Y2K since people were thinking that everything was

Sandee Kastrul
President & Co-founder,
i.c.stars

Favorite Innovation:

The abacus: a calculating tool used in ancient centuries before the adoption of the written numeral system.

"You can do really complex math on an abacus, and it is such an old innovation. It is about the symbols, the placeholders, and what is possible. You can make one for your kids with cheerios."

Best day of my career:

"It was after 9/11, after the dotcom exploded, and the other co-founder had left. We had no cash, only three employees, and our board said it was over. I made Erik pinky swear that we wouldn't quit, and we wouldn't acknowledge anything other than hope."

i.c.stars has since given hundreds of inner city people access to tech careers and unprecedented salary growth.

going to explode, clocks would stop, and elevators would cease to work."

While the clocks kept ticking after Y2K, the tech bubble that had been formed did not, and as Sandee recounts, the bubble burst of the early 2000s left both a hole and an opportunity. "When the bubble burst, there was such an energy of sadness and grief in Chicago." But that sadness didn't last long, as Kastrul continues, "Y2K transcended the startup community. It spurred this growth of consultants and tech service providers who were going to bring solutions to the table. That was the start of something much greater; how do we bring solutions to the table for everyone, enterprise customers, startups, etc." Sandee is describing the beginning of a monumental shift in how innovation and entrepreneurship were viewed at large.

The turn of the century brought a new venture for Kevin Willer and Ted Souder, who at the time had just started the Google office in Chicago when the dotcom bust had left many tech companies in the dust. "We opened a Google sales office at 401 N. Michigan Ave. in a shared office space," states Kevin Willer. "At that time, people were saying, 'why would we need a search engine?'" The dotcom bust paved the way for entrepreneurs to leverage a new and exciting technology to solve problems and create new value. Two years later, the Chicago Innovation Awards began, with the goal of highlighting the breadth of innovation occurring across industries in this diverse city. It reflected the need to shine a spotlight on all of the amazing innovations that were going on here, and not just for people like Kevin and Ted – for all new, impactful solutions regardless of technological sophistication.

Fast-forward to today, and things have swung in the other direction. Large corporations have not only brought down the drawbridge over their moats, but they are actually going out and trying to rub shoulders with the now successful entrepreneurs. They aren't the only ones that are collaborating to bring an innovative culture to the forefront of the city. The globally top-ranked incubator, 1871 is a poster child for entrepreneurial success in Chicago. The space was created by the public and private sectors coming together to build an entrepreneurial ecosystem for tech-startups.

"The scene has totally changed," says Jai Shekhawat. "There were no playbooks then. The state of the ecosystem in Chicago now has become robust, and all of us who have figured it out have become stronger."

The Benefit of Innovation

Innovation is defined as creating and capturing new value for customers, consumers, citizens, or constituents – whomever the end-user or recipient of the value is. It can come in a variety of forms: new or improved products, new services, processes, systems, programs, and new business models. There is disruptive innovation, which tends to displace other existing businesses and establish a new status quo (like Uber relative to the taxi industry), and there is incremental innovation which tends to add benefits, features, or attributes to products, programs, or services that currently exist. It also means applying a current technology or process to a new market or industry. As the global economy becomes more and more knowledge-based, future growth will come from organizations' success with innovation.

Innovation drives economic growth through generating revenue and creating new jobs. It is as simple as that. If people started recognizing this reality, every city and country would be focused on building an environment that sustainably propels new innovations forward. As the economy becomes increasingly knowledge-based, digital, and service-oriented, innovators and entrepreneurs will reach new heights. Their importance as key economic drivers, as well as indicators of future trends and emerging opportunities, will mandate that cities cultivate a culture that encourages innovators, fosters their growth, and supports them directly.

Innovation does not happen by itself. It is not a sport for a single player; innovation is a team sport. There are only so many sages like Bill Gates and Steve Jobs who are able to create billion-dollar businesses in their garage, and they are few and far between. Despite this, the number of new businesses and social innovations being created on a daily basis is surging in Chicago. The reason: they are surrounded by an innovation ecosystem.

What Is an Innovation Ecosystem?

An innovation ecosystem is a culture, mindset, and supportive community that enables multiple people and organizations to

Terry Savage

Nationally-syndicated
finance expert and author

work together in launching or scaling a new business, product, service, or business model. Chicago has created, or rather, an innovation ecosystem has emerged and evolved in Chicago over the past roughly twenty years. To Kristi Ross, the Co-CEO of tastytrade, the ecosystem is comprised of five pillars: "It is the same five pillars that withstand the test of time: startups, large corporations, universities, venture capital, and government. They all play a key role in building and reinforcing the ecosystem." Additionally, a sixth key pillar is the nonprofit sector, which devotes countless resources to advancing the causes, services, and businesses of others.

The Chicago innovation ecosystem has not come from one person taking the lead, but rather a shared leadership approach where many individuals, startups, incubators, universities, politicians, corporations, nonprofits, foundations, and the like have come together in a way that has started to connect the dots. Has the city reached a pinnacle of innovation achievement? No, of course not; it still has a way to go. But there has been a noteworthy groundswell in Chicago that supports innovators, entrepreneurs, and tech talent.

As Terry Savage, the nationally recognized financial columnist, states, "The essence of innovation and entrepreneurship is that it enables you to change direction and create your own life in a different way going down a different path."

The Burgeoning and Diverse Chicago Innovation Economy

The current Chicago innovation ecosystem is described by John Flavin, who recently led the University of Chicago's Polsky Center for

Entrepreneurship and Innovation, as "the combination and alignment of small companies and startups, venture capitalists, large corporations, students and universities, service providers, law firms and the like." Indeed, connectivity is spreading and strengthening.

The innovation ecosystem in Chicago is diverse, not just in types of organizations but in industry as well. The former Chief Information Officer for the City of Chicago and the State of Illinois, Hardik Bhatt believes, "It's diversity and how all of the different sectors are working together that differentiate Chicago from other cities. We haven't put all of our eggs into one basket." Chicago does not depend upon one or two industries to uphold its economy like other cities do. The benefits of this are twofold: it buffers the overall economy to better withstand significant industry decline, and provides opportunities for businesses and entrepreneurs of all types.

Chicago in and of itself mirrors a highly diversified portfolio. The players of the ecosystem are many, and they range from companies both big and small, to governments, universities, venture capital firms, nonprofits, incubators, and both public and private sectors. It is a wide-ranging mix of influencers. But what makes the city unique is that somehow over the past twenty years, these various components have come together to develop a comprehensive ecosystem in which each has a role to play. As Shivani Vora, Managing Director of the Accenture Innovation Hub, explains, "What sets Chicago apart from other markets is our ability to think together across businesses, civic organizations, and startups. That is the formula for success."

As of 2019, Chicago has been ranked first among U.S. cities in new and expanding corporate relocations for the past six years.

Shivani Vora

Managing Director, Accenture's Innovation Hub

Fun Fact:

Shivani has visited more than forty countries, but still chose Chicago to call home. Shivani is the leader of Accenture's first Innovation Hub, tasked with providing clients a comprehensive resource for accelerating internal innovation.

Large corporations are coming in droves to mingle with the tech startups and entrepreneurs that have been cultivated. In fact, a record 351 companies expanded or relocated to Chicago, resulting in over $2 billion in investment and over fourteen thousand new jobs. As Ed Wehmer, President and CEO of Wintrust states, "Chicago has always benefited from its geographic location. There is a reason why we have grown to be the twenty-first largest economy of the world based on GDP. It is totally diversified, and that wouldn't have happened if all of the ingredients and attributes weren't here. You have sea, rail, and air – all of which connect cities throughout the U.S. and beyond. And the benefit and reinforcement of diversification continues."

The companies that are coming to Chicago reflect the diversity of the economy as well. "We're revolutionizing the insurance business, the financial services businesses, data analytics, and logistics businesses," cites Michael Krauss, the former Co-chair of the Mayor's Council for Technology Advisors and Co-founder of Market Strategy Group. Technology and innovation are not industry specific; they are relevant in all forms of business, which is why an industrially diverse region is the perfect place to build new technologies. As an example, one of the first-ever master's programs in artificial intelligence was recently launched at Northwestern University by Narrative Science Co-founder, Kris Hammond. AI was embedded in nearly 20 percent of all 2019 Chicago Innovation Award nominations, and is one of many types of technology that are being integrated across industries.

Remarkably, Chicago has the most diversified economy of any other American city; no one industry employs more than 12 percent of the total workforce. The implications of this are that innovation cuts across sectors and industries. The past 310 Chicago Innovation Award winners are a textbook example of this. The awards highlight companies that have developed unique, innovative products, services, or businesses that have achieved tangible impact in the marketplace. Among the slew of winners there is a diverse portfolio ranging from healthcare and fintech to food and industrial products. This is the rich ingredient that makes an innovation ecosystem: a diverse economy that thrives with large companies and small startups. This diversity provides traction for innovation to happen.

Diversity of industry is only one piece of the puzzle, however. Many cities have great entrepreneurs and talent, but Chicago also has a culture that brings it all together. As Michael Krauss affirms, "We are collaborative and friendly in Chicago. We are not as rude or arrogant as others have a reputation for in other cities. We are every bit as competitive, but we tend towards collaboration. We want to win. We have a lot of very successful first-generation immigrants."

The spirit of collaboration goes back to Chicago's roots, back to the fire of 1871 when people had to band together to survive and rebuild the city. "We even turned the river around," cites Andrea Zopp, CEO of World Business Chicago. She recounts, "People respond, 'You did what?!' The destruction of the fire brought the city to a point that required making connections." According to Ed Wehmer, "After the Chicago fire, you saw many ethnicities show up to rebuild – the Poles, Germans, Irish, Greeks, Hispanics – they saw the need to work together. This is how we have evolved into the quilt that we are right now: the Midwestern melting pot."

What Makes Chicago Unique?

Competition is what fuels capitalism and inspires businesses to innovate, and it has a monumental effect on how businesses think about growth. In the same vein, now more than ever, cities need to recognize the threat of competition and discern their unique strengths that can distinguish them from other competitive regions. The purpose is two fold: to attract and retain talent.

Developing, training, and retaining the workforce is vital to the growth and maturation of a city. Without it, the core infrastructure weakens; with it, a city can soar. In order to do this, cities and regions need to establish themselves as hubs for business, innovation and jobs. Chicago, like any big city, has its problems and challenges, but one of the largest is its public image. Al Capone no longer lives here; he died over seventy years ago. But we still are often referred to in his light, and unfortunately it can be difficult to speak about Chicago without bringing up the "elephant in the room." These are serious issues that need to be discussed and in time solved, but there can and should be more than one story at a time.

Chicago also has a "Second City" image to overcome, especially when compared to places like San Francisco and New York. But, the attraction of the Coasts is changing, a key driver of which certainly being the cost of living. In the Valley, affordable real estate is sparse, labor is more expensive, and transportation time is increasing. And while indeed Silicon Valley may still be the hub of technology startups in the country, Chicago has developed a breadth of innovations across a variety of industries that creates opportunities for all who are willing to work for it.

According to financial guru Terry Savage, "Chicago has always been innovative. Maybe it's something in our water or maybe it's our cold weather. But whatever it is, the cornerstone of Chicago is resiliency! People here are resilient."

One of the main responsibilities of Andrea Zopp, CEO of World Business Chicago, is to showcase Chicago on a global scale. Her work is focused around bringing people to the city and demonstrating all that it has to offer with the hopes that they will bring business. She often tells visitors, "We have it all: great neighborhoods, great schools, beautiful parks, amazing theatres and restaurants, great sports teams, great businesses, and great universities." It is an impressive mix, but these have been here for quite some time. Something unique has happened during the past two decades to accelerate the best of Chicago's attributes and bring them together.

"Openness and accessibility are what make Chicago unique," cites Hedy Ratner, the Founder of the Women's Business Development Center. Chicagoans open doors for one another, and have a set of values that are based on this openness and collaboration. There is a clear viewpoint that innovation is a team sport, as opposed to something done individually. People trust each other in Chicago that the intention is to do well by others rather than harm them.

When Brian Bannon, the former CEO of the Chicago Public Library, moved to the Midwest seven years ago from the West Coast, he soon discovered the ease with which he was able to find a role he could play in the ecosystem. "What I saw here was a more diverse mix of people who made you feel wanted. Seattle is notorious as a city that, if you move there as an outsider, it can be tough to break in. As the saying goes, 'Seattleites are the friendliest people you'll never know.' Not the case in Chicago."

At the end of the day, it's a difference in culture, as Matt McCall describes: "It's so competitive in Silicon Valley that collaboration really isn't the culture there. There is more of a feeling of FOMO (fear of missing out). Who's getting the bigger deals? There is more of an allure to get the really big whatever. It is not characterized by pulling community together." Competition versus collaboration is a delicate balance, and neither is right or wrong. The difference is, where Silicon Valley's strength lies in its dog-eat-dog edge, Chicago's innovation ecosystem finds strength through working together.

"If you think about the Bay Area, you get a lot of ego and mercenary behavior," reflects Taylor Rhodes, the former CEO of Chicago unicorn startup SMS Assist. "There, I am basically focused on how to increase my value until the next startup or unicorn wants me. So, you go through a lot of ego-driven interactions with people. It is also a culture where you need to prove that you are the smartest person in the room. Most people there are sniffing you out to see how intelligent you are." For the West Coast, this has obviously worked well. They have created an unmatched culture of technology entrepreneurs and the numbers don't lie.

It's a different kind of success that Chicago has seen grow over the last two decades. The mindsets of people have shifted towards innovation and entrepreneurship with a renewed sense of possibility, and it has happened in a way that has leveraged the many strengths of Chicago's business culture. As Terry Savage believes, "Everything evolves." This is certainly true for Chicago's innovation ecosystem. Over the past twenty years, the city has undergone a transformation that has stimulated innovators and entrepreneurs more than ever before.

Taylor Rhodes

CEO, Applied Systems

Former CEO, SMS Assist

Best day of my career:

"The day that RackSpace crossed $2 billion in annual revenue. It wasn't because of that number, it was because of all the things it represented. It represented a triumph over a lot of barriers that many companies fail to reach, and having to re-figure out how to matter in the post-Amazon world."

The San Antonio-based company was eventually bought by Apollo Global Management in 2016 for $4.3 billion.

CHAPTER

3

HOW THE ECOSYSTEM EVOLVED

CHAPTER 3: HOW THE ECOSYSTEM EVOLVED

Traditionally Innovative

When considering major historical milestones of Chicago, it becomes abundantly clear that innovation has been a deep-seated value of its residents for generations. It takes a special kind of mindset to reverse the flow of a river in order to stop pouring waste into the main water source. Completed in 1900, the flow of the Main Stern and South Branch of the Chicago River were reversed by using a series of canal locks thereby increasing the flow from Lake Michigan into the river. Even by the year 1900, Chicagoans were accustomed to taking big steps to solve big problems.

Twenty-nine years prior, Chicago was destroyed by the devastating fire of 1871. And yet, Chicagoans rebuilt the city. While the people were downtrodden, they were determined. The "Great Rebuilding" was the collaborative effort to construct a new urban center, complete with big businesses and innovative buildings that embraced a new style of architecture.

As Chicago continued to grow, the question of housing surfaced. Where would all these people live? The solution was the skyscraper, invented in 1885 with the completion of the ten-story Home Insurance Building peaking at 138 feet. Brian Bannon, the former CEO of the Chicago Public Library underlies the cultural significance of the steps taken by Chicago's innovators: "We are a city that has contributed in a meaningful way to the culture of our country and our world. Many of the ways that people think about America, foods, music, art, and even the skyscrapers, can be traced to Chicago."

From architecture and civil engineering to logistics, energy and food, Chicago's history is laden with inventors and innovators blazing trails in their respective industries. Armor and Swift expanded the reach of the beef industry with their launch of refrigerated rail cars, and Marshall Field's reinvented consumers' shopping experiences with the advent of the department store. In 1942, the first human-made self-sustaining nuclear chain

Michael Krauss

Co-founder,
Market Strategy Group

Favorite Innovation:

The Twinkie

Best day of my career:

*"The day I met
Tom Kuczmarski."*

Tom Kuczmarski is the
co-founder of Chicago
Innovation, president of
Kuczmarski Innovation,
and co-author of this
book.

Fun Fact:

It's not uncommon to
hear Michael referred to
as "the most connected
guy in the city."

reaction was initiated in Chicago: Pile-1, the world's first nuclear reactor. Even the Twinkie was invented in Chicago back in 1930. Innovation has found a home in Chicago for centuries, and this is seen through a gradual inclination towards technology and entrepreneurship.

Industrial Roots Bear Innovative Fruit

Chicago has always had innovation in its DNA. Relentless renewal and practical invention are front and center of what makes Chicago unique. In 1909, the city released the Burnham Plan: an integrated series of projects including new streets, parks, rail and harbor facilities, and civic buildings, all with the goal of making large-scale improvements to the city and its citizens. Daniel Burnham, to this day, is best known for his admonition, "Make no little plans." The shape and infrastructure of the city today can be traced back to this plan. As Michael Krauss, Co-founder of Market Strategy Group, says, "We have a history of innovation. It's a continuous innovation ecosystem that goes back to the founding of Chicago." The culture of Chicago has always been centered around innovation, but for a long time that mindset was sheltered behind closed doors and ivory towers of large corporations.

By the 1930s, Chicago had become a manufacturing town. At this time, the Chicago industrial area was the second-largest manufacturing area in the U.S. behind only New York City. Chicago represented large-scale, capital-intensive, heavy industry; however, other industries from clothing to printing and publishing, banking, automotive, and food and beverage found success as well.

Entrepreneurship was a cornerstone for the Chicago economy's post-depression recovery, but these ventures quickly rose to the ranks of large companies. In 1955, the first McDonald's opened in the Chicago region, and the Second City comedy troupe went live. The first of the Playboy Clubs were opened in 1960. The John Hancock building was built in 1969, followed shortly thereafter, in 1973 by the construction of the Sears Tower, the tallest building in the world at the time. The growth of Chicago's ecosystem has indeed been an evolution, but one that has had innovation as a river running underneath it for more than a century.

The 1970s, 80s, and 90s brought more and more growth to large corporations like Walgreens, United Airlines, Motorola, and Exelon. But silos were beginning to be built, not on farms but within the city. In fact, most large corporations were headquartered in the suburbs outside the city limits.

Sam Yagan

CEO, ShopRunner

Former CEO, Match Group

Fun Fact:

In 2013, Sam was named to *TIME Magazine's* "100 Most Influential People in the World" list, and in 2014 was listed as one of *Fortune Magazine's* "40 Under 40".

Early Beginnings of Today's Innovation Ecosystem

Entrepreneurship doesn't need to start in a garage. Howard Tullman, a serial Chicago entrepreneur, describes how the majority of new ventures largely used to come from corporations: "We had a business community where a lot of entrepreneurial people were living within the confines of large corporations. The idea that you would go out and just start up your own business was pretty radical." Moreover, when Sam Yagan, the CEO of ShopRunner, moved to the Midwest in 2007, he felt "it was a very siloed ecosystem. Big companies just didn't talk to little companies."

The following year, the 2008 recession displayed a different kind of motivator for entrepreneurialism: necessity. As Kevin Willer, another Chicago tech pioneer who now runs the venture capital firm Chicago Ventures, recalls, "Starting with 2008, a bad year for the economy, the tech scene started to rise in Chicago. Many people lost their jobs and went to start their own companies. Entrepreneurship actually became a good opportunity, as opposed to the less-than-desired alternative." People were starting to see that they had more control over their destiny than they did in a large corporation, and they began to like this newfound freedom.

It is a different place today than it was a decade ago. "Today, the Chicago innovation ecosystem is vibrant; it's alive and stronger than ever before," states Kristi Ross, Co-CEO of tastytrade. To make such a drastic change happen, it needed to become clear to people that entrepreneurship outside of a corporation was a viable option in Chicago. It took a major success to show others that it was possible, and for many in the "Second City," that success was Groupon.

When the CEO Andrew Mason was only 26 years old, he, Eric Lefkofsky and Brad Keywell had established Groupon as one of the fastest-growing tech companies in history. Many Chicagoans can recount their reactions to hearing that they had turned down Google's offer to buy them for $5.75 billion. It was a turning point as people began to realize that they didn't have to be running a major-sized company to find success in business. Amanda Lannert, CEO of Jellyvision, shares how influential Groupon was to entrepreneurs like herself: "They were the real defining factor in making it seem possible in Chicago. Groupon showed that you could go from zero to IPO (initial public offering) almost instantaneously."

While acquisition wasn't the path for Groupon at the time, big exits have continued to fuel the perception that entrepreneurs and tech founders are able to create significant wealth, achieve high growth, and bring new jobs into the city. In 2014, Fieldglass was acquired by SAP; one of the few times a high-growth tech company had been sold for over $1 billion in Chicago. Soon after, Cleversafe was acquired by IBM for $1.3 billion in 2015. The transaction created eighty millionaires in Chicago among the former equity-owning employees.

People were not only starting to understand the potential of entrepreneurship in Chicago, they were beginning to reap the benefits. As more and more people took notice of the downstream effects of successful innovators and entrepreneurs (such as seeing eighty new millionaires walking around), they started to be more intentional about fostering the ecosystem that connected one another.

Defining the Chicago Innovation Ecosystem

An innovation ecosystem describes the composite and diverse participants and resources needed for innovation to occur at a regional level. Through a combination of collaborative pathways between companies, entrepreneurs, tech startups, universities, nonprofits, governments, and more, the innovation ecosystem is a network of activities and opportunities to create and support new business. An innovation ecosystem represents an environment where people cannot only think of innovative solutions, but can take action to realize their vision. While traditionally, ecosystems focus on investments and structures that encourage innovation, in Chicago, it is more about creating a culture and a relationship-building capability that garners a supportive and highly interactive community.

In Chicago, the essence of the innovation ecosystem is collaboration. This is an important distinction that keys into the uniqueness of the ecosystem Chicago has developed in contrast to other cities and regions. The ecosystem has evolved in such a way because of a business culture where people seek out connections to others rather than maintaining a purely competitive mindset.

Competition exists, but the mindset is "who can solve this problem best," as opposed to "me vs. you." As Caralynn Nowinski Collens, former CEO of manufacturing technology hub MxD, explains, everyone in the ecosystem is competing for the same goal: "It is a robust and complicated community, but all in all we're trying to increase our overall competitiveness and put Chicago on the map as a place for technology innovation to flourish." When entrepreneurs and innovators as a whole are supported by others, their ideas and concepts can more easily flourish since they have access to the resources they need to move things forward.

The Chicago innovation ecosystem describes the cultural underpinning of the community of innovators and entrepreneurs that has grown over the last two decades, as if it were a regional incubator. What had begun as a few individuals coming together

Harper Reed

Former CTO, Obama for America

Former Head of Commerce, Braintree

Former CTO, Threadless

Favorite Innovation:

The mobile phone

"The digital divide is more about access to broadband than about access to computers. Also, the phone presented this opportunity where we can create apps. I do have a payphone in the backyard that connects to Japan though."

Best day of my career:

"The best day was winning an election that put me on the map."

Harper was the CTO for Barack Obama's 2012 re-election campaign.

to try and foster an environment that was supportive of entrepreneurs with capital, talent, guidance, education, mentoring, and the like, has developed into something much more. As Harper Reed, respected Chicago tech entrepreneur and former Head of Commerce at Braintree, describes, "We emerged from the minors and now we're a major league team, making real returns to investors and participating in the venture world in a new way."

What is the Chicago way? It is a belief or mindset that innovators work hard, solve real world problems, collaborate with others, and give back. Each of these are important components of the ecosystem. Relationships are a key element of the success formula, and the energy continues to build.

One reason why various types of organizations are so capable of working together in Chicago is that the city has the most diverse economy in the country, and this is what tends to foster more of a collaborative mindset. Whether it is because technologies are transferable across industries, or because B2B solutions are relevant to all types of companies, organizations within the region have an ingrained mindset to help each other more than compete against each other.

Universities and Venture Capital

Universities have long made a conscious effort to engage in real-world discovery, research, and teach business practices, but the recent shift in business culture has led to a shift in mindset at academic institutions as well. Linda Darragh, faculty at the Kellogg School of Management, says, "When it came to Kellogg, we realized that we needed to teach entrepreneurship completely differently. In 2012, we started from scratch, and we realized that creating the right courses would require us to have real-world practitioners as faculty; people who had done it." Business and innovation were becoming further separated from academic theory and more closely aligned with what worked in the real world. By getting the practical experts into the classrooms, universities were starting to train the next round of innovators.

In 2013, the University of Chicago founded the Chicago Innovation Exchange, now the Polsky Center, as an incubator for University of Chicago students and residents of Hyde Park and surrounding communities. "I came on board to start the Chicago Innovation Exchange," says John Flavin. "There was a whole wave of students who were interested in entrepreneurship, even more so than finance. By bringing an incubator to campus, we were able to foster more interest in innovation."

One of Chicago's key strengths upon which the ecosystem is built is its massive university and academic base, and schools like the University of Illinois at Chicago, Loyola, DePaul, and others have all realized the need to not only teach innovators but connect them with their surrounding ecosystem. A great example is Illinois Tech's Accelerated MBA program, where as a part of their tuition, students become members of Chicago Innovation, giving them the chance to attend monthly events and engage in real world learning with innovators. In turn, students affiliated with Chicago Innovation are able to receive a scholarship of twelve thousand dollars.

While universities provide invaluable educational resources to aspiring

Kevin Willer

Partner, Chicago Ventures

Former Founding CEO, 1871

Co-founder, Google Chicago Office

Favorite Innovation:

Chicago's approach to building a tech community

"We have all banded together to build the infrastructure. It hasn't been any one person or any one thing. It has just been a lot of good work, and ultimately we all benefit from it."

Best day of my career:

"I thought it was a treat to meet the British Prime Minister when he came through here at 1871."

entrepreneurs, it is the venture capital community that brings tangible resources to the table. Chicago used to be a fly-over city relative to venture capitalists; it has now become a fly-into city. As more capital is being invested in startups than ever before, the number of exits and serial entrepreneurs continues to grow.

But it has not always been this way. The growth of venture capital firms in the Midwest is relatively new. As Kevin Willer recalls the origins of his firm Chicago Ventures, "When we started in 2013, we realized there wasn't much capital here and there were a lot of startups." In addition to Kevin's group, there were only a few other venture investors, including current Governor, J.B. Pritzker. Since that time, however, the amount of venture capitalists has greatly increased, due largely in part to the ecosystem of support around budding entrepreneurs. As one of Pritzker's partners, Matt McCall says, "There are twenty-something management teams that have grown to over a billion dollars in revenue. Then, they in turn become angel investors." Continues Sam Yagan, who began his own firm Corazon Capital after finding success co-founding OkCupid, "The running joke now is that everyone has a fund here. But the impact of these funds is to provide more capital to the once capital-starved ecosystem."

Chicago's capital situation, much like the innovation ecosystem as a whole, is far from reaching its peak. There is still room to grow, and it is growing rapidly. This increase in funds is largely thanks to an economy that yields frequently successful startup exits, many of whom had entered at the incubator stage.

The Rise of the Incubators

Incubators and accelerators have changed the startup landscape of Chicago. They have contributed to the collaborative spirit of the region. An incubator, when run effectively, can be viewed as a miniaturized version of the broader innovation ecosystem. They establish small communities of innovators and entrepreneurs interested in advancing their ideas, and often provide resources to help them achieve their goals.

Incubators bring innovators together in a supportive way to give entrepreneurs creative places to work and build their ideas, and that's not just for independent founders. Even large companies are looking for ways to connect with these incubators, often by building offices within their walls to "rub shoulders" with the innovators on a daily basis. There are now over 120 different incubators in Chicago. Ten years ago, there were none. As Sam Yagan puts it, "They have exploded onto the scene and play a key role in developing the next generation of startups." Not only do they play a pivotal role in developing startups, the incubators have differentiated themselves in a way that aligns with Chicago's industrial diversity.

With an extremely diverse industrial base comes an industrially diverse set of new startups, each with unique needs and varying growth rates. For this reason, many incubators have specialized to various industries. 2112, for example, aims to provide services to entrepreneurs in the film, music, and creative technology spaces. The Hatchery Chicago enables local entrepreneurs to build and grow successful food and beverage businesses. mHUB is the Midwest's leading physical product innovation center, and is changing the way companies and entrepreneurs think about digital manufacturing.

Healthbox, run by Nick Rosa, is a healthcare accelerator, which operates out of Sandbox, a venture capital firm. MATTER is another healthcare startup incubator and corporate innovation accelerator that brings together entrepreneurs, scientists, investors, and clinicians dedicated to improving the health of everyone. The list goes on and on, and while these incubators play an important role in supporting entrepreneurs, they are just one piece of the ecosystem puzzle.

While Chicago has traditionally always been innovative, the recent growth of an innovation and entrepreneurial ecosystem has been an extra boost to the business community. It shows the impact and result of individuals and organizations of all types pulling together and connecting with one another for the good of the city and for the good of entrepreneurship and innovation.

CHAPTER

4

THE SECRET SAUCE: COLLABORATION

CHAPTER 4: THE SECRET SAUCE: COLLABORATION

Chicagoans Collaborate

The business culture of every city is steeped in challenges, issues, and conflicting objectives. Each type of organization, from small startup to large corporation, university, government institution, or nonprofit has a set of priorities, goals, and barriers that it must keep top of mind at all times to stay afloat. Every element within a city's innovation ecosystem has unique needs that can lead to a self-focused, competitive, and often-conflicting set of actions. It is easy for each player in the game to argue why their needs should be satisfied first. But what many don't realize is that these needs are often different, and what one person lacks, another has in surplus.

This is what makes Chicago's innovation ecosystem different; it recognizes this distinction. It has a civic-minded culture, made up of people who are interested in and care about the growth and success of their community. It is all about making the place they live and work better, and understanding how they can play a unique role in contributing to that greater mission.

There is a value of collaboration that transcends the competitive mindset. This culture of collaboration means that people in and across organizations work together to complete a task or achieve a goal. Teams that work collaboratively often are stronger and more effective than the individual who is fighting for something on his or her own. But collaboration requires relationship building to be the core underlying skill needed for it to work. Without that, collaboration is merely a process rather than a behavior shift.

Connection Making and Personal Relationship Building

Connection making is a fundamental ingredient of collaboration. Whether it be in search of new clients, a business partner, or even a mentor, people all over the ecosystem are actively looking to expand their networks and connect with one another. Sam Yagan,

Marc Shiffman

President & CEO,
SMS Assist

Best day of my career:

"Achieving a billion-dollar valuation at SMS Assist, because I started as the most junior guy on the team. I proved to myself that I had actually acquired all of the skills along the way to bring a group of people together to get a remarkable achievement."

With this valuation, SMS Assist became one of a handful of Chicago-based unicorn companies.

Founder of SparkNotes, Vice Chairman of Match.com, and CEO of ShopRunner; understands the direct impact he can make simply by connecting with new people. "Just yesterday, I had three meetings where I talked with entrepreneurs who were seeking advice or help," he cites. Yagan is representative of how many Chicagoans who have found success are open and willing to help others. They want to help. They want to see the startup community grow, prosper, and succeed. Yagan continues, "I think folks feel a sense of obligation or desire to really help Chicago succeed."

Brian Bannon, the former CEO of the Chicago Public Library, corroborates Yagan's assessment: "It goes back to breaking through the artificial barriers that exist in some cities, where people don't feel comfortable introducing you to senior level people." Bannon elaborates on the uniqueness of Chicago's business culture of collaboration: "When I first moved here, there were people making lots of connections for me, and now I feel the same responsibility to make connections for others. It directly contributes to the cross-pollination of the innovation ecosystem." Bannon's comments reveal that Chicagoans embody the value of collaboration so much that they perceive it as a responsibility to fulfill and foster.

Bannon is currently running the New York Public Library system and it may be fair to say that he will not find the same level of collaboration there. He states, "There is a culture of collaboration in Chicago that is really welcoming to newcomers and outsiders. There is a real pressure to contribute in a meaningful way to give back to Chicago." And not all cities are like this.

Before his time at SMS Assist, CEO Marc Shiffman spent his days where Brian is now:

New York City. He recalls the level of impersonality he felt from others there: "In New York, no one takes time for anything or anyone. I lived in the same building for twelve years, and as I'm moving out, the woman two doors down says to me, 'Oh my, you must be the new guy moving in.' I say, 'No, actually I am the guy moving out who has lived here for over a decade.'" Of course, the culture of an entire city of 8.6 million people can't be defined by a single impersonal neighbor. However, Marc's experience speaks to the heart of the differences in the value Chicagoans place on connections and personal relationships.

Indeed, the culture of Chicago's business community stands alone in contrast to the coasts. But what is the benefit of this collaborative nature? How does a friendlier atmosphere inspire innovation success? As Matt McCall puts it, the sense of community inspires people to collectively work together to solve large-scale goals: "Everyone's in it together. There's no sense of divisiveness. People help pull each other up." It's not just meeting one another; it's helping provide resources and share ideas.

Gaining Insights from Collaboration

Another essential element of collaboration is leveraging personal relationships for the exchange and development of new ideas. Linda Darragh, professor at the Kellogg School of Management at Northwestern University, reinforces, "If you don't network and build relationships, you miss out on many of the resources and information that help create successful entrepreneurs." By furthering relationships, the secret sauce of collaboration further propels the ecosystem forward.

Ed Wehmer

President & CEO, Wintrust

Favorite Innovation:

The microwave

"You can make a hot dog in a minute. Popcorn in no time. I think the microwave is one of the best."

Best day of my career:

"The day in 1980 that I got married to my lovely wife. I really out-kicked my coverage on that one."

In addition to learning from others on an individual level, plugging into the ecosystem at the organizational level is another great way that Chicago companies promote the collaborative culture. Ed Wehmer, the Founder and CEO of Wintrust Financial, recalls, "When I started the bank, the concept was that you had to get involved with the community. That was just part of the deal, but it is also the fun part. You meet people and make new relationships, and you continue to grow." Ed believes that anything that a person can do to make the community better makes him or herself better. "It was good business for us," he says, "Wintrust's whole business model was founded on the importance, value, and widespread adoption of collaboration in Chicago." This is a key insight about why people and groups decide to collaborate; it is mutually beneficial to get involved, and it's a much harder road to go alone.

Organizing Around Collaboration

The concept of collaboration is fluid and intangible; it can be hard to understand at a theoretical level. If searching for concrete examples of collaboration in action, one should look no further than a banner institution in Chicago: 1871, the world's number one business incubator. Founded in 2012, the incubator was established with the goal of creating a community of startups. Their intention wasn't just to build an office space for small tech companies, they wanted something more.

They managed to create a micro-ecosystem of collaborators including universities, large corporations, community leaders, and investors who learn from and work with each other to create an interactive and collegial environment supporting entrepreneurs. As Kristi Ross, Founder and Co-CEO of tastytrade, explains, "They have representation of all pillars of the ecosystem. It really is about the community and people coming together to make that happen." 1871 proved to many in Chicago that when people across the business spectrum come together, big things are possible.

Collaboration by definition is a team sport. It requires a group of people working together with the intention of helping one another achieve a mutual goal. For many, connection making and networking are terrific ways to grow and develop ideas. For others with a grander vision of the future, it takes organizing under a single entity to make systematic change happen. A textbook example of this type of collaboration is a project that started in 2018 called P33, whose goal is to create a tech plan for the city to reclaim Chicago's position as the world's center for technological discovery and development.

As the CEO of P33, Brad Henderson, cites, "The mission of this group is to strengthen a diverse, inclusive, and flourishing technology community in Chicago." P33 refers to a plan for 2033, a century after the Chicago World's Fair, where once again the city will be able to showcase its technology on the world's stage. Comprised of business and nonprofit leaders from across the private sector, the group's goals include keeping tech talent in the state, increasing capital to Chicago-region startups, and enhancing the connectivity between startups and larger Chicago corporations. It epitomizes the underlying mindset of collaboration that makes Chicago unique, and the potential that comes from bringing people together under a single rallying cry.

Another critical group in the formation of the ecosystem was the Chicagoland Entrepreneurial Center started by David Weinstein. Jerry Roper, who was at the time leading the Chicagoland Chamber of Commerce, Andy McKenna, President of DirecTech, and Jim O'Connor Jr., Managing Director at William Blair & Company, took recommendations from the Mayor's Council of Technology Advisors (MCTA) to create a single portal for entrepreneurs, as well as a startup fund. This was how the Chicagoland Entrepreneurial Center (CEC) and I2A fund were born. The CEC started the $10 million seed fund in 2007 to provide early-stage funding to startups at a time when little capital was available locally.

Kristi Ross

Co-CEO & President, tastytrade

Fun Fact:

Kristi Ross was the co-host of the 2017 Chicago Innovation Awards, a role she assumed after having been a winner on the same stage three years earlier for tastytrade.

It was truly a group effort to establish a substantial organization around supporting entrepreneurs when people like former and current Governors Pat Quinn and J.B. Pritzker; Steven Collens, then a VP at the Pritzker Group and now the CEO of healthcare incubator MATTER; Dan Lyne, former technology director for World Business Chicago; Matt Moog, who founded the tech social-networking site, Built In Chicago; and 1871's first CEO Kevin Willer came together with other leaders to make the CEC a possibility.

At the helm of the Chicagoland Chamber of Commerce, Jerry Roper was committed to innovation, entrepreneurs, technology, and bridging the components of the ecosystem together. He formed a focal point where other organizations mobilizing around innovation and entrepreneurship could go for support. David Weinstein, Founder of the CEC, recalls being introduced to some of the first groups connecting the dots: "I remember when Tom Kuczmarski and Dan Miller came to visit us at the CEC and told us about the Chicago Innovation Awards. We started having meetings, and I got the Illinois Technology Association and Illinois Coalition (now the Illinois Science and Technology Coalition) involved. I saw all of the initiatives as a chess board where each moved strategically to enhance the overall city." Through the efforts of organizations like these, businesses and entrepreneurs in Chicago have been able to acquire the resources and connections necessary to grow their ideas.

Collaboration Within the Public Sector

The private sector isn't the only area that believes in the importance of connecting people together. Hardik Bhatt, the former Chief Innovation Officer for the City of Chicago and the State of Illinois, now leads Digital Government for Amazon's Web Services. When thinking back to his government days, he recalls the desire from the public sector to keep up with the pace of private businesses: "We wanted to hear from everyone and make sure everybody else knows what is going on throughout the ecosystem. If Tom Kuczmarski is hosting the Chicago Innovation Awards, we've got to be there because it's a great way to spread the word about the amazing work being done in Chicago. It is another way to collaborate." Hardik summarizes this value so well: "Collaboration is as much a benefit as it is an expectation or responsibility in Chicago."

But groups operating in the public sector aren't just peering down on the business community; they get their hands dirty as well. The Mayor's Council of Technology Advisors was started in 1998 under Mayor Daley. The goal was to bring together different elements of the community to help the government collaborate with businesses. The Council was started by Mayor Daley and David Weinstein, who was the Special Assistant to the Mayor for Technology at the time. The two were quickly joined by Beth Boatman, CIO for the City of Chicago, and Steve Mitchell of Lester B. Knight & Associates. The group brought leaders from the public and private sectors together to share important news, partnerships, milestones, innovations, and more from the various corporations and startups across town.

Soon after, others would take the mantle of co-leading the group, such as Katherine Gehl, who inherited the position of the Mayor's Special Assistant for Technology; the subsequent CIOs of the City, Chris O'Brien and Hardik Bhatt; and Michael Krauss, Co-founder of Market Strategy Group. Howard Tullman, a serial entrepreneur and former Executive Director of the Kaplan Institute at Illinois Tech, describes the significance of this group: "I think the MCTA was the first instance when you'd have scruffy entrepreneurs and leaders from large companies all at the same table. It was only possible because of the Mayor bringing everyone together." This initiative started a unique dialogue among different levels of the ecosystem that had previously never communicated, and could not have happened without Mayor Daley reinforcing the importance of innovation and collaboration.

Just as a diverse team of developers can create a better product than a team of like-minded individuals, an organization centered around connecting disparate elements of the ecosystem builds a greater impact. As Hardik Bhatt elaborates, "The reason we have gotten so much more connected in Chicago is because we had groups like the Chicago Innovation Awards, the MCTA, the CEC, the Illinois Technology Association, and the Illinois Venture Capital Association." Building on Mayor Daley's focus on making Chicago more of a tech and innovation hub, Mayor Emanuel took it all to the next level with a high degree of support and involvement to build an entrepreneurial and innovation-funded city. Today, Mayor Lori Lightfoot is working hard to inspire economic development within underserved neighborhoods of the city, and part of this will need to involve supporting innovative new businesses in those regions.

"Chicago's fabric of connections is part of the DNA of the city, and it helps people support and interact with one another. It makes for stronger companies, more confident entrepreneurs, a more vibrant community, and a local government that wants businesses to succeed, generate jobs, and fuel economic growth," summarizes Kristi Ross.

Collaboration Is a Necessity

Matt McCall cites, "What defines Chicago is its strong sense of community. Everyone is in it together. There is no sense of divisiveness. People try to help each other out – to help pull each other up." This connectedness that has formed among the business community isn't just a nice group of friendly people; it is a critical element of what keeps the innovation ecosystem in balance. Matt continues, "The one thing that would cripple the ecosystem is if we started moving from 'we' to 'I.'"

As Matt alludes, the Chicago business community can't grow to become a top-tier innovation hub as a series of disconnected silos. It must be done as a unit. But thankfully, by investing in relationships and helping one another achieve their goals, this spirit of community and collaboration continues to stay top of mind.

It might seem counter-productive to favor collaboration over competition in a business environment, and it only works when everyone is on board. How does someone even begin to overcome a natural tendency to compete over collaborate? The easiest way to convince people that it works is through proof. "One of the reasons that 1871 has thrived is because people come in and actually see the interaction that produces creative partnerships and education partnerships," says Andrea Zopp, CEO of World Business Chicago. Once they're on board, she continues, "people naturally want to help. Collaboration is in our history and culture. Fellow CEOs want to help you get integrated into the community and become a part of it."

Collaboration is a core value that guides the culture of Chicago's innovation ecosystem, but it is not the only one. There is a set of shared values across the region's business community that distinguishes Chicago's business culture from other cities, and guides the ways in which people and organizations work with one another.

CHAPTER

5

THE
C.H.I.C.A.G.O.
WAY

CHAPTER 5: THE C.H.I.C.A.G.O. WAY

Collaboration only works when a similar vision, purpose, and goals are agreed upon by participants. Underlying this agreement is an intangible force that connects people together to form a powerful culture, and at the heart of this culture are the values of the individuals.

It became abundantly clear from the innovators and entrepreneurs that molded and led Chicago's innovation ecosystem that there exists a unique set of core principles that has guided the city's unique business culture. These values underpin the attitudes that permeate Chicago's innovation community, enabling like-minded people to come together and do great things. Collaboration is the vehicle through which people are able to advance one another's ideas, and is a key cornerstone for driving the culture forward. Values are the core beliefs that explain how people partner with one another and why. These principles are unique to this city, and as such are defined as "The C.H.I.C.A.G.O. Way," summarized as:

- **C**ity Pride
- **H**umility
- **I**nclusion
- **C**alculated Risk-taking
- **A**ltruism
- **G**rit
- **O**penness

Taken together, these principles serve as a powerful catalyst for economic growth through innovation.

City Pride

Why are Chicagoans willing to spend four months out of the year in an unforgiving wintry climate, trudging to work against icy, twenty mile-per-hour winds in five layers of clothing? Talk to most anyone in Chicago and their attitude toward the city is likely the same: people love this city and their allegiance to it runs deep.

There is a pride that people in Chicago have for their city that powers a boisterous "coming together" of entrepreneurs, investors, corporate leaders, academics, and others who are quick to tell people that Chicago is a city on the rise. Taylor Rhodes, a transplant to Chicago who arrived in 2016 after presiding as CEO during the $4 billion sale of Rackspace, notes that there is a way about Chicagoans that keeps them yearning for more. "People here will always tell you the Chicago story and why the city deserves to be better regarded than it is. They've got a little bit of a healthy chip on their shoulder to go prove something."

Maria Wynne

CEO, Leadership Greater Chicago

Fun Fact:

In 2019, Maria was named one of *Crain's Chicago Business'* "Chicago's Most Powerful Latinos". Maria was also the co-host of the 2019 Chicago Innovation Awards.

In a real sense, Chicago is one of the leading global economic powerhouses. Its GDP is greater than many countries. But at the same time, there is an underdog quality to Chicago's status as a hub for innovation. Perhaps it's because the city is sandwiched between the oft-idealized epicenter of the financial world, New York City, to the east, and the pedestal-topping technology capital of Silicon Valley to the west.

People in Chicago's innovation community are aware of the "fly over city" remarks at venture capital conferences on the coasts. They scoff at them. Chicagoans are proud people, and there is a lot to be proud of these days. Every time a new Chicago startup is acquired or a new corporation relocates to Chicago, people from the mayor all the way down to local students are ready to share the news. As Maria Wynne, CEO of Leadership Greater Chicago, explains, this is a universal movement among people in the community to share stories and create impact. "We convene, we connect, and we mobilize leaders to affect positive change in the region." Those stories spread and serve as a powerful magnet to attract new people, capital, and businesses to a city that yearns for more.

Pride fosters a sense of shared purpose. It is the glue that stitches together a community. As Ed Wehmer, President and CEO of Wintrust Financial, describes, "People understand the concept of community, and I think they're used to relying on each other to put the barn up, so to speak." There is a delicate balance between pride and ego, and thankfully most Chicago innovators fall on the former side of the equation.

Humility

"Humble, hungry, and smart." These are the words that were hung on huge banners on the walls of SoCore Energy, a Chicago startup under the leadership of Pete Kadens until it was sold to Edison International in 2013. While humility is one of those traits most people admire, it's not always the first word used to describe CEOs running corporate offices. As outlined in *Apples Are Square: Thinking Differently About Leadership,* co-authored by Tom and Susan Kuczmarski, many CEOs today still exhibit a "command and compete" style of leadership as opposed to the more collaborative approach that puts egos in check.

On the whole, leaders who have found success in Chicago's innovation ecosystem take a humbler approach to leadership. Some may call it "Midwestern niceness," however the truth is that most people who have ascended the ranks in Chicago's business and technology community are some of the most genuine and modest people around.

Matt McCall, longtime Partner at one of the most active venture capital firms in the Midwest, Pritzker Group Venture Capital, notes the pervasiveness of this behavior among Chicago's innovators. "We're now seeing these billion-dollar exits from people who are maintaining their humility. Look at Jai Shekhawat from Fieldglass or Chris Gladwin from Cleversafe. Mike Gamson at Relativity or Kevin Willer, who started the Google office in Chicago and then became the first CEO of 1871. Person after person, they each pass the 'I'd like to go to lunch with them' test."

A sense of humility fosters genuine and honest relationship building: a critical activity for any innovator who knows that innovation is achieved through a diverse and cross-functional team. No one can go it alone. Innovators need others to support them, believe in one another, and share their social capital to help others become more successful. Part of this means humanizing one another, and getting to know colleagues on a personal level. Marc Shiffman, CEO at Chicago tech unicorn SMS Assist, notices that people in Chicago's technology community innately want to share their personal lives. "When you talk to people here, they're immediately talking about themselves, what they do, and their families. They're giving you the full picture of how they became them and what they care about. It's this sense of wholesomeness that exists in Chicago. People take the time to get to know each other."

Low-ego leadership is visible among Chicago's business elite, serving as a role model to others who aspire to reach similar heights. Brian Bannon, former CEO of the Chicago Public Library, spent many years in San Francisco's tech community before coming to Chicago. "One thing that is different about Chicago compared to other tech ecosystems is the fluidity of how people move between class circles. It doesn't matter if you're a billionaire. Less attention is paid to your social ranking; there is more interest in what you have to bring to the table."

Strip away someone's perceived self-importance and all that remains is substance. Chicagoans seek out people who are rich in substance and humble enough to demonstrate that character is what matters.

Brian Bannon

Director, New York Public Library

Former Commissioner & CEO, Chicago Public Library

Best day of my career:

"Chance the Rapper was a kid at Jones High School when he did his first mix-tape at the library and got famous. A couple years ago, we met together and he asked to do an open mic night at the library. It was great that he wanted to come back."

Inclusion

Chicago is a city built by immigrants, and these roots manifest within the culture in the form of a place where inclusion can thrive. People often describe Chicago as a city of neighborhoods. Seventy-seven distinct neighborhoods, in fact, each with its own identity and residents hailing from various origins, religions, and ethnicities. But having different kinds of people in the same city does not equate to inclusion.

Tribal attitudes of "me vs. you" can segregate a city and push people away as opposed to bringing them together. This is something that cities all over the world have struggled with for centuries. Make no mistake; Chicago is not perfect in ensuring that all kinds of people are participating in its innovation economy. As Jai Shekhawat, Founder of Fieldglass, puts it, much of Chicago is "like a salad bowl: together but separate." Unfortunately, few cities today can claim that people of all genders, races, ages, and socio-economic backgrounds are being provided with equal opportunity for success. But, the leaders of Chicago's modern entrepreneurial movement are actively embracing inclusion as a core tenant of progress. Jai continues, "We need to meet people where they live," and that is exactly what today's innovation ecosystem is working to do.

In 2016, Mayor Rahm Emanuel appointed Andrea Zopp as the city's first-ever Chief Neighborhood Officer to ensure that the far-reaching neighborhoods of Chicago were being given the opportunity to plug into the resources that were fueling tech growth in the central business districts. As CEO of World Business Chicago, the leading business development arm of the city, Andrea adopted a motto of "inclusive growth" to describe its focus on future activities.

While there is still room to grow, Chicago has made big strides in supporting female entrepreneurs in particular. In October of 2018, *Crain's Chicago Business* reported that Chicago boasts a higher percentage of female startup founders than any other city in the country. While change is taking root now, the seeds for female business ownership in Chicago were sown long ago, with the heft of the credit going to Hedy Ratner, Founder of the Chicago-based Women's Business Development Center (WBDC). To date, the WBDC has had over eighty-five thousand women participate in their entrepreneurship-focused training courses, and in 2019 won a Chicago Neighborhood Award at the Chicago Innovation Awards for their ScaleUp program which helps women grow their small businesses.

But inclusion involves much more than supporting women. Chicago-based Bunker Labs is one of the nation's leading incubators for veteran-owned businesses. Blue1647 is a network of coworking spaces and accelerator programs focused on African American entrepreneurs. The Illinois Hispanic Chamber of Commerce relocated its offices to startup incubator 1871 to push Hispanic entrepreneurs further ahead. Programs are popping up in Chicago to support the LGBTQ community, Asian Americans, various under-represented religious groups, and other communities that were previously disconnected from the center of Chicago's technology ecosystem.

Chicago Innovation has adopted "Innovation is for Everyone" as its anthem for the city. Chicago is indeed a salad, though the chefs of the city are realizing that the ingredients are better together than apart.

Calculated Risk-taking

People in Silicon Valley often talk about "moon shots," the idea of swinging for the fences to chase a big idea that no one has ever done before. Concepts that will change the world forever. In Chicago, people don't often talk about "moon shots." Mike Gamson, CEO at Relativity, elaborates, "We love 'doubles' in Chicago. The seven-year company that got up to $120 million and sold to someone, we're like 'amazing, great job!' In San Francisco, that's an abject failure." Some have criticized that this greater sense of risk-aversion among Chicago entrepreneurs is a handicap compared to Silicon Valley entrepreneurs. Through conversations with dozens of successful Chicago innovators, one can fully appreciate that there is a subset of risk-taking that does indeed thrive in Chicago: *calculated* risk-taking.

To return to Mike's baseball analogy, Chicago's entrepreneurs hit a lot of singles, doubles, and triples. In contrast, the coasts have significantly more strikeouts littered with occasional home runs. Neither of these approaches are inherently correct, but understanding the culture of the startup and venture ecosystem provides a better understanding of the different rationales. Gamson elaborates, "Who am I to say what is right or wrong? I think the beauty of entrepreneurship is that you get to decide whatever you want for yourself." At the end of the day, runs win games and there are many ways to put points on the board. Calculated risk-taking is what leads to Chicago's victories.

This sense of pragmatism should not be confused with anti-innovation principles. On the contrary, being pragmatic is at the root of innovation; timing is everything. Pragmatism forces the need to understand customer pain points, wants and needs to create the right solutions. The "calculated" in "calculated risk-taking" means identifying and proving there is a need in the market. As a result, Chicago's innovators are hyper-focused on creating new products and services with revenue-generating business models that focus on the customer from day one.

Kevin Willer, Partner at Chicago Ventures, one of the most active seed-stage technology venture capital firms in the Midwest, flies all over the country meeting with entrepreneurs. He has experienced firsthand the value of pragmatism as a principle that leads to results. "Chicago is unique in that our entrepreneurs are more pragmatic. Some people would say that we don't think as big as people in the Valley, but we are more realistic about expectations for building a business."

What Kevin is getting at is the calculated nature of the risks that Chicagoans lean on. People aren't willing to take a chance on an idea unless it makes sense and has a clear path to growth. He continues, "We want revenue earlier on, and we want to show real value. We also tend to disrupt older industries, so we see a lot more B2B (business to business) than B2C (business to consumer). It might take longer to get to success, but at the end of the day we build real companies here."

Silicon Valley can have their consumer-focused apps. That's not where Chicago's entrepreneurs generally decide to play. "Our strengths are real businesses," says Harper Reed, former CTO of Threadless, who later went on to lead digital marketing efforts in the Obama for America campaign. "No one here makes 'Facebook for dogs.' We start out with something that makes money or has a semblance of something that will make money. That's something that is unique to Chicago versus Silicon Valley."

Perhaps it's because Chicago's innovators are so ingrained in their problem-solution mindset that they cannot help but look around them and examine how they might be able to help others. Rather than turn a blind eye to those in need, Chicago's leaders are motivated to act. It is precisely this type of customer-focused and methodical revenue-building mindset that led Chicago to become number one in the country in venture capital returns of ten times or more in 2017 and 2018, according to PitchBook.

Howard Tullman, longtime serial entrepreneur who has started over a dozen high-growth tech companies, knows that Chicago's approach to risk-taking pays off. "No one in Chicago will ever spend $300 million and hope it works out. What characterizes us is that we're not afraid to fail, but we're smart enough to say that our strategy is to build businesses that can exit." Howard hits the nail on the head; innovation requires stepping outside of one's comfort zone, but there is a difference between taking risks and being reckless.

Altruism

Like any well-oiled machine, for an innovation ecosystem to march forward there must be a reinvestment of fuel back into the system. This reinvestment can take many forms. "Many people give different types of currency. People invest money, but they also invest time," says John Flavin, CFO of Endotronix, Inc. and Chicago biotech entrepreneur who led two successful IPOs.

Of course, plowing money back into new startups is a very effective tool for stimulating economic growth and keeping the cycle of entrepreneurship humming along. Many successful entrepreneurs redistribute portions of their earnings into the next wave of budding startups, and when successful, they reap the benefits of their investments. The motivation here is purely capitalistic; people invest money into lucrative opportunities for their own personal wealth creation. But one of the strengths of Chicago's innovation ecosystem is another type of motivation that is perhaps even more powerful: successful entrepreneurs becoming philanthropists.

The idea of "giving back," whether it's people's time, expertise, or philanthropic dollars, is woven into the culture of Chicago's innovation community. In fact, in Chicago it's an expectation. Sam Yagan notes, "There's a real willingness to support the greater good. There's a civic mindedness in the business community here rooted in our history. I thought that all cities have it, but as I've learned more about the various civic institutions in Chicago, I think it's something special here."

Dating back to the turn of the twentieth century, regional economic development has been a central component of the Chicago business community's DNA. As previously mentioned, the city-altering Burnham Plan of 1909 was created by members of the Commercial Club of Chicago. The group of leaders came together to create a plan to change the landscape of the region, building highway and railway systems, parks, lakefront attractions, and more. Their legacy of locally engaged activism is seen a century later through organizations like P33, which is hoping to create a similarly impactful impression on the city with their tech plan.

It might at first seem ironically braggadocious to laud someone's altruism and modesty as their defining strengths, but it truly is a significant character trait found in the entrepreneurial community. Successful startup founders know that they haven't achieved their success alone. Each entrepreneurial story involves, at some point, the interjection of another person who provided the much-needed advice, mentorship, and helping hand, often at the most critical or desperate times. That's why so many entrepreneurs are ready to give back and pay it forward, and how altruism has become a focal point in the community culture.

Matt McCall has seen this cycle of Chicago-based entrepreneurs giving back to support the innovation ecosystem. "We're now in a fourth generation of successful Chicago entrepreneurs. There are so many people who have been successful here. Then, they turn around and religiously give back to the community." Matt continues with a few notable examples: "Take Mike Gamson, who previously headed up Chicago's LinkedIn office and is now CEO of legal tech startup Relativity. He gets up in the morning and thinks about how he can invest in the community in a meaningful way through his time and mentorship. Or look at J.B. Pritzker, Chris Gladwin, Jai Shekhawat and Kristi Ross. The number of times someone has a major exit and then turns around and gives it back to the Chicago community is mind-boggling. I'd argue it's unsurpassed."

Kevin Willer has observed similar behavior. "Folks in Chicago want to help out the next generation of entrepreneurs. They sit on boards, mentor, and support economic development initiatives. The spirit of giving back to other Chicago companies has been passed down from multiple generations of Chicago business leaders. You are told that when you have success, you have to be philanthropic when you can."

Some opposed to coining this as "altruism" will be quick to point out that even charitable giving is to an extent done for self-interested gain. They will say that entrepreneurs giving back to others is done in order to achieve some measure of return on investment, whether it be a gain in status, recognition in the community, or some other self-centered motive. But Ed Wehmer, Founder of Wintrust Financial, will be just as quick to naysay the naysayers. "I don't want to hear about ROI, that's not why we do it. We don't go out and pat ourselves on the back. We're doing it to make the city better. Getting involved is simply the right thing to do." Ed goes on to say, "If you look at the charitable contributions from Chicago, they are better in terms of the number of charities supported and the benefits gained. There's more money given to charity in the Midwest than the East and West Coasts per capita."

This "giving back for the sake of giving back" attitude is pervasive in the Chicago region. The philanthropic nonprofit sector is incredibly robust. According to the National Center of Charitable Statistics (NCCS), Chicago has a significantly higher density of nonprofits compared to its two large U.S. city peers, New York City and Los Angeles. In its most recent survey, the NCCS noted that Chicago boasts 14.54 nonprofits per ten thousand people; that's nearly 40 percent more nonprofits per capita in Chicago than either coastal city.

For better or worse, the desire among Chicago's business leaders to support their local community is matched, if not exceeded, by the number of opportunities to roll up one's sleeves and get involved. This supply and demand equilibrium of "giving back" generally leans towards demand, and the next step is to connect-the-dots. As Holly Copeland, Head of Corporate Social Responsibility at Horizon Therapeutics, details, "People need to respond to the demands that

Holly Copeland

Senior Director of Corporate Social Responsibility, Sustainability & Impact, Horizon

Former Deputy Director, Office of Entrepreneurship, Innovation, & Technology for the State of Illinois

Favorite Innovation:

The Internet

"I believe the Internet can be the great equalizer. Regardless of where you come from, you can change your circumstances if you have access to the Internet."

Fun Fact:

In addition to her accomplished career in both the public and private sector, Holly found time to co-write a children's book with her two daughters: *Teca: The teeny, tiny teacup pig & her BIG world.*

are made. For the most part, the population that needs the most focus is voiceless. No one is advocating for them; they don't have high-paid lobbyists, and they don't donate to political campaigns."

The Millennial generation, which is among the most socially minded that the U.S. has ever seen, will soon make up the nation's ranks of business leaders. As Ed Wehmer shared, these values are passed along from generation to generation. So, it's no doubt that Chicago will be well positioned to capitalize on this spirit of altruism for years to come.

Grit

> *"Chicago is edgy. It's rough and tumble. It's the city that works."*

John Flavin, CFO, Endotronix, Inc.

"The city that works" is a popular Chicago phrase coined by Mayor Richard J. Daley, who presided over the city from 1955 to 1976. This slogan added to Chicago's narrative as a working-class city, founded by immigrants who embraced hard work. What causes this work ethic to persist, and why is it still prevalent in Chicago? It comes down to two things: the cold, and the capital (or lack thereof).

Akin to how an organism must adapt to its surroundings to thrive in a biological ecosystem, an innovator in Chicago must learn to adapt to external realities in order to achieve success in the innovation ecosystem. A cold hard truth in Chicago's environment is that it's a very chilly climate. The city is tied for second most days per year when the temperature drops below 0°F. "The cold weather keeps us sharp," Tom Kuczmarski, Founder of Chicago Innovation, likes to say. But it does more than wake people up in the morning, it reinforces the necessary trait to survive in Chicago: Grit.

Sandee Kastrul, Founder of i.c.stars, a nonprofit that trains low-income adults to enter the technology workforce, sees grit as a must-have trait to live and work in Chicago. "Grit enables you to see things through. Chicagoans see things through. If we aren't a people that sees things through, we would never last a Chicago winter."

Although few cities experience -30°F polar vortexes, there are plenty of cold cities across the country. Cold weather alone cannot account for Chicago's entrepreneurs being a particularly pluckier bunch than most. There's much more to this story.

In juxtaposition to its large U.S. city counterparts, Chicago annually sees less venture capital investment. According to *Bloomberg*, Chicago received $1.53 billion in venture deals in 2017, ranking the city seventh in the U.S. despite being the third largest city in the country. Compare this to San Francisco and New York City, which received over $19.6 billion and $13.3 billion respectively, and one can see that there is a significant gap.

People are often quick to point out the negative implications of such a large discrepancy – less capital means less money to invest in new ideas. But many business leaders will remind skeptics that investment capital is the second-best kind of capital a company can receive. The best form of capital comes from customers' pockets. Amanda Lannert, CEO of Jellyvision, elaborates: "The type of 'VC' that Chicago is best at nailing down is 'Vested Customers.' We get customers early on to fund ideas before we even get that private capital." Revenue-generation is the primary focus for Chicago entrepreneurs, and is what guides their pragmatic and dogged pursuit of business models that work.

A lack of capital leads to resourcefulness, a scrappy mindset common among Chicago's innovators. As Mike Rothman, Chairman and Founder of SMS Assist, shares, "As a thirty-five-year entrepreneur, I have learned that the harder you work, the luckier you get." Much like the cold weather, nothing makes an entrepreneur sharper than the realization that the only way to grow their business is by lifting themselves up by their bootstraps and finding a way out. That's the idea behind "bootstrapping," a term of pride in the startup

Mike Rothman

Founder & Chairman of the Board, SMS Assist

Co-founder, Theron Technology Solutions

Fun Fact:

Mike Rothman founded SMS Assist, which won a Chicago Innovation Award in 2012 before going on to become one of the city's unicorn companies with a valuation over $1 billion.

community. It refers to growing a business without fat checks coming in from venture capitalists to keep the ship afloat until cash from customers kicks in. There's even a popular online talk show called *Bootstrapping in America* produced by tastytrade that celebrates gritty entrepreneurs. To no surprise, this show is filmed in none other than Chicago, Illinois.

Chicago's entrepreneurs don't have the luxury of sitting down at a coffee shop where angel investors and entrepreneurs are mingling at virtually every table. That's a scene out of Silicon Valley. Chicago's mythology is different. Carl Sandburg captured Chicago's ethos in his 1914 poem titled "Chicago."

> *Hog Butcher for the World*
> *Tool Maker, Stacker of Wheat*
> *Player with Railroads and the Nation's Freight Handler;*
> *Stormy, Husky, Brawling*
> *City of Big Shoulders*

Today's innovators in Chicago are much more focused on technology stacks than wheat stacks, but the values in the city's workforce remain the same. Andrea Zopp sums it up, "We have an incredible core work ethic. People here are not afraid of hard work and they are willing to put that in. That effort, of course, underpins all kinds of innovation." Chicago's innovators don't give up easily. If they did, they wouldn't be around to see the spring.

Openness

In a time when some political leaders across the country and the world are putting up both figurative and literal walls with their calls for stricter rules on immigration, Chicago has followed a different path. It is a path that the city has followed since its founding as a welcoming place for people from all over the world.

Under its Sanctuary City policy, Chicago does not enforce federal immigration laws. In 2018, when President Trump threatened to withhold $5 million in federal funding for Chicago's police force unless Chicago abandoned its Sanctuary City policy, Chicago's Mayor Rahm Emanuel filed and won a lawsuit against U.S. Attorney General Jeff Sessions, enabling the city to keep its Sanctuary City policies and uphold its commitment to openness and inclusion.

This story illustrates a principle that the city has never wavered from: Chicago is open to everyone. This trait is strong among Chicago's innovation community, because the leaders within it know that growth comes from both retaining talent, capital, and businesses, and *attracting them from elsewhere.*

Transplants to Chicago who bring new ideas and energy into the ecosystem have experienced this warm welcome from the business community. Experts on innovation know the importance of diversity of thought. A community needs people with different skill sets, backgrounds, experiences, and viewpoints to provide the multiple perspectives needed to solve complex problems. Chicago is a city built on this principle, which is bolstered by the kindness of strangers.

"When I came to Chicago from New York City, I didn't know many people in business here," recalls Marc Shiffman, CEO of SMS Assist. "I immediately encountered kindness and lots of open doors. People were willing to talk to me and connect me with others. Chicago is such a welcoming place."

Brian Bannon, former CEO of the Chicago Public Library, experienced something very similar. "When I first moved to Chicago, I developed friendships that I knew would be lifelong within the first six months. It took me the full seven years that I was in San Francisco to have the same number and quality of relationships." Like many newcomers to Chicago, Brian also felt a responsibility to continue the cycle of openness. "One other part of the culture here is how everyone follows through on connecting you to others. When someone asks me for a connection, it is easy to say 'sure' and then not follow up. But in this town, you don't wait for someone to ping you. You make it happen and make the introduction."

Taylor Rhodes, CEO of Applied Systems, remembers that there were "no shortage of really open and generous people here who were willing to spend time with me, give me their honest opinions and sincere offers of help." Tracing back to the narrative of wholesome Midwestern values being as real as the winds coming off Lake Michigan, the people who excel the most in Chicago's innovation ecosystem are genuinely nice, honest, open people.

The kindness inherent in Chicago's innovation community plays a vital role when new people arrive, like recently graduated students and foreign-born entrepreneurs. Transplants to a new city often arrive anxious. They don't know anyone. They are alone. This is when the authentically nice people shine. They welcome newcomers with a smile and an outstretched hand. Those people are the scouts and ambassadors of Chicago's innovation ecosystem, encouraging newcomers to join the community and making it stronger one member at a time.

The C.H.I.C.A.G.O. Way

Every person has their own unique sets of values and beliefs. They have their own strengths and weaknesses. The same can be said about a community of people. What has worked for Chicago's innovation community – a focus on **city pride, humility, inclusion, calculated risk-taking, altruism, grit and openness** – could indeed be a prescription for other cities. It has surely worked for Chicago, enabling a culture to take shape. These values reinforce desired behaviors of people within Chicago's innovation community, strengthen its culture, and ultimately build a foundational set of principles that Chicagoans believe will keep paving the way forward.

While the development of an ecosystem is certainly a group effort, there are without a doubt individual leaders who played integral roles in building Chicago's innovation ecosystem. In addition to embodying the aforementioned values to their core, they have been examples of what it takes to achieve success through innovation and entrepreneurship, and to this day act as role models for how a single person can play an outsized role in their community.

CHAPTER
6
THE INDIVIDUALS

CHAPTER 6: THE INDIVIDUALS

Chicago's innovation ecosystem was collectively built through an almost infinite number of actions from an uncountable number of people. To use the phrase, "it takes a village," would be too literal in describing what has transpired in terms of the growth of innovation and entrepreneurship in this region. But as Sam Yagan, Founder of Excelerate Labs and CEO of ShopRunner, concedes, "There were moments, events, people, and companies that had these outsized impacts."

While group efforts and collaboration were key growth factors in the ecosystem, it's necessary to illuminate people whose outsized impacts were crucial to the building of Chicago's innovation community. This story simply cannot be written without recognizing the efforts of certain individuals. To be clear, there are countless other unnamed individuals who played vital roles; what's unique about the people in this chapter, however, is that they were cited numerous times by this book's interviewees as outliers. The research showed that these individuals were deserving of special attention because they have served as role models and inspirational leaders to many people in the city. "We are human; we look to leaders," says Michael Krauss, Co-founder of Market Strategy Group and an active connector who contributes to many civic-focused tech initiatives. "It helps to have some really terrific leaders who are successful. People who we like and admire."

Entrepreneurial Visionaries

In August of 2010, *Forbes Magazine* featured a cover story with the title, "Meet the Fastest Growing Company Ever." The article was not about Facebook, Google, Apple, Amazon, or Uber. The accolade of "Fastest Growing Company Ever" was bestowed upon a new startup out of Chicago known as Groupon. At the time, it was the fastest company in history to reach a $1 billion valuation. "Groupon put Chicago on the map," stresses Marc Shiffman, CEO of SMS Assist. "And that was because of Brad and Eric."

For over 25 years, **Brad Keywell** and **Eric Lefkofsky** have been business partners responsible for some of Chicago's most-talked-about tech successes. In addition to being the co-founders of Groupon, they teamed up to launch two additional companies that have gone public: InnerWorkings, a tech-based marketing firm, and Echo Global Logistics, a transportation brokerage firm. Brad also founded Uptake, a multibillion-dollar data analytics startup focused on solving complex industrial problems. Eric founded Tempus, a multibillion-dollar startup that is using data to improve cancer treatment outcomes. Their venture capital fund, Lightbank, has invested in successful Chicago tech companies, such as restaurant industry disruptor Fooda, publicly traded social media company Sprout Social, and Drivin, which allows car dealers to better manage their inventory.

Erik Gordon, associate clinical professor at the Ross School of Business at the University of Michigan, where Brad and Eric attended university, once said, "For them to still be friends and stay together, it's sort of a Hewlett and Packard situation." Each are very active civically and philanthropically, from Eric serving on many nonprofit boards, to Brad's founding of Chicago Ideas, a community-focused "ideas platform for everyone."

Another Chicago entrepreneur tied to multiple outsized successes is **Chuck Templeton**. Chuck is most known for being the founder and former CEO of OpenTable, an online reservation platform for the restaurant industry that he launched in 1998, took public, and later sold to Priceline Group for $2.6 billion. "I aspire to be Chuck," notes Sam Yagan. "He started a great business, and invested in and mentored a bunch of others." Chuck served as the Founding Chairman of Grubhub, and also mentored and invested in Braintree and Cleversafe, a pair of business-to-business technology companies that also reached a $1 billion valuation status. "Chuck is one of the best early-stage investors around," says Troy Henikoff, former Managing Director of startup accelerator Techstars Chicago and an early-stage investor at MATH Venture Partners.

Chris Gladwin, Founder of Cleversafe, is another Chicago tech entrepreneur who is often cited as a key player in the city's innovation scene. Cleversafe, a data-storage creator, was Gladwin's third and most successful tech startup. "He is the biggest thinker in Chicago," exclaims Harper Reed, who spearheaded technology efforts at Braintree, Threadless, and the 2012 Obama for America campaign. "He doesn't do small projects, and he finishes what he starts." As previously mentioned, in selling Cleversafe for $1.3 billion to IBM in 2016, Chris created eighty millionaires who were employees at the company. This is one of his greatest points of pride. He encouraged

Jai Shekhawat

Founder & Former CEO, Fieldglass

Favorite Innovation:

The bicycle

"It's simple, can carry you long distances, is easily repaired, is good for your health, and makes you happy."

Best day of my career:

"The day I announced the sale of Fieldglass to SAP. I stood in front of the employees at 8:28am. It was scripted to the minute and my admin was there with the finger over the button to be pushed at 8:30am."

In 2010, Jai Shekhawat sold his company Fieldglass to SAP for over $1 billion.

these employees to share the wealth by starting their own ventures, and many did.

It's this cycle of entrepreneurship that shows how one person can impact a whole community. Chris has remained very active in building Chicago's technology community, through a $7.6 million donation to help Illinois Tech strengthen its computer science department, along with creating P33, a civic organization aimed at taking Chicago's technology prowess to the next level.

Jai Shekhawat founded Fieldglass, which he sold for $1 billion to SAP in 2015. Jai has invested in and mentored many Chicago startups, including logistics company FourKites and social media advertising firm UPshow. Hardik Bhatt, who leads Digital Government at Amazon Web Services, highlights the value Jai brings to companies in Chicago: "We evolve because the people are staying here and reinvesting. Jai Shekhawat is on a dozen boards and is investing in companies." Thankfully, Jai plans to stay local. "I love this city and will continue to live here. I will likely add to my civic duties, and will continue mentoring other entrepreneurs," he says.

Mike Rothman founded SMS Assist, one of Chicago's unicorn startups that got its start by bringing technology to the commercial property maintenance industry, and then found further success by serving large residential property owners. It is one of the city's largest and fastest-growing venture-backed businesses, having already raised over $250 million from the likes of Goldman Sachs and Pritzker Group Venture Capital. The company reached a key milestone by employing over one thousand people by 2019, and continues to expand its footprint throughout the country. Since transitioning from CEO to Chairman of SMS Assist, Mike has had more time to give back and invest in the Chicago innovation community. Through Theron Technology Solutions, Mike and his son Alex became the Founding Diamond Sponsor of Chicago Innovation to help further stimulate innovation throughout the Chicago region, and in 2018 Mike acquired Technori, one of Chicago's most active startup platforms and online media companies.

Matt Maloney founded one of Chicago's most successful startups, Grubhub. It was one of Chicago's recent startups to reach decacorn status: a company valued at over $10 billion. Grubhub has long served as a role-model company for many in the city, demonstrating that it is possible to create a decacorn-level organization in Chicago.

Tom Sosnoff hit it big when he sold thinkorswim to TD Ameritrade for over $600 million in 2009. He joined forces with his former CFO **Kristi Ross** as Co-CEOs of tastytrade, an online financial firm. Kristi and Tom have also been very active in nurturing Chicago's fintech ecosystem. Their online talk show, *Bootstrapping in America* gives an audience to the next generation of entrepreneurs hoping to share their stories and solutions with the community.

Genevieve Thiers, an early Chicago tech pioneer of the 21st century, has been dedicated to fixing the imbalance of women in technology. She founded Sittercity.com in 2001, the country's first company to take caregiving services online. Since then, Genevieve has mentored hundreds of entrepreneurs and invested in over ten female-led tech companies.

Sam Yagan showed his entrepreneurial chops at the age of twenty-two when he sold his first company, SparkNotes to Barnes and Noble. He went on to be the founder of OkCupid, which he later sold to Match.com, and soon afterwards was invited to take the helm of the Match Group as its CEO. In 2009, Sam and fellow entrepreneur, Troy Henikoff teamed up to launch Excelerate Labs, Chicago's first significant accelerator program for startups, which later became Techstars Chicago. Sam then became CEO of e-commerce company ShopRunner, and in doing so, pulled off something quite noteworthy. "Sam was the first person to relocate an entire technology company from Silicon Valley to Chicago. He's very proud of that," notes Chicago Ventures Partner and former CEO of 1871, Kevin Willer.

David Kalt is another serial Chicago entrepreneur who experienced major success in both his first and second acts. Founded in 2000, his online brokerage OptionsXpress went public and eventually brought David a $1 billion sale when it was acquired by Charles Schwab in 2011. An avid lover of music, he used some of his earnings to buy local guitar shop Chicago Music Exchange. Quickly seeing there was a better way to buy and sell used music gear, David launched Reverb.com in 2013, which he sold to Etsy for $275 million in 2019. David maintains a focus on using his company's success to help those in need, which he does through Reverb Gives' programs that provide musical instruments to under-resourced schools across the world.

Amanda Lannert is an outspoken force of nature for technology entrepreneurship in Chicago. After joining Jellyvision in 2000, she has taken this interactive software firm to new heights, continuously winning "best place to work" awards. Amanda is also highly active in bolstering Chicago's startup community, having served on the advisory boards of several organizations, including digital tech incubator 1871, The Starter League coding boot camp, the Illinois Technology Association, and as a member of ChicagoNEXT, a civic group focused on entrepreneurship and economic development.

Healthcare is a domineering industry in Chicago's diverse regional economy, employing the largest share of the workforce at 12 percent. **Glen Tullman** is one of the most notable healthcare entrepreneurs that has risen from Chicago over the past several decades. As Founder and CEO of Allscripts, Glen took the healthcare IT company to over $1.4 billion before going public. His next firm, Livongo, is revolutionizing chronic disease care management. Livongo raised $235 million in funding before Glen took it public as well. He also launched a $100 million healthcare-focused venture capital fund, 7Wire Ventures, in 2018. In doing so, Glen's focus has been to bring innovation to the entire healthcare ecosystem by identifying, investing in, and scaling startups that are driving change in the industry.

Pete Kadens demonstrates the versatility that lies in some of the city's most dynamic entrepreneurs. After founding and exiting his solar energy startup SoCore Energy, Pete moved on to the ever-changing cannabis industry by becoming CEO of Green Thumb Industries, the second U.S. cannabis company to go public. Meanwhile, Pete remains very active philanthropically, focused heavily on alleviating poverty. He is the Chairman Emeritus of *StreetWise*, a publication that uniquely provides homeless individuals with a chance to gain economic self-sufficiency through selling newspapers, and has recently launched his own foundation to drive change in Chicago's social impact sector.

When it comes to Chicago entrepreneurs who have achieved significant success, the list goes on, and on, and on. Frankly, half of this book could be profiles of Chicago entrepreneurs, but entrepreneurs alone do not make an innovation ecosystem. Though many of these trailblazers bootstrapped their way to entrepreneurial success, there is a key group of people in the ecosystem that have devoted their careers to helping lay fertile soil so that innovation could take root.

Community Connectors and Cheerleaders

A city of siloed innovators and entrepreneurs working independently of one another may lead to the growth of individual companies, but the growth of an ecosystem requires interconnectedness. Chicago's rise as an innovation hub is rooted in deep collaboration among stakeholders. That's why it is crucial to highlight people who played vital roles in convening innovators, along with pointing out those who celebrated the important work occurring in Chicago's innovation community. These community connectors and cheerleaders helped to propel innovation forward.

Among the first watering holes in Chicago's innovation community was Mayor Richard Daley's Council of Technology Advisors, spearheaded by **David Weinstein**. In running the MCTA, David regularly hosted sessions that allowed different leaders of the Chicago innovation, technology, and entrepreneurial communities to come together. Many meetings would have upwards of twenty different speakers, each one given the floor to inform the group for a minute or two about their organization's current efforts. Over time, David passed on the leadership of the group to others, including **Michael Krauss**, Co-founder of Market Strategy Group. For years, the council remained a powerful way to stay in the know and build bridges with other leaders.

"Few people have experienced the breadth and depth of Chicago's innovation scene as David Weinstein," wrote Kate MacArthur in a November 2014 *Chicago Tribune* article. As the Founding President of the Chicagoland Entrepreneurial Center,

Dan Miller

Co-founder, Chicago
Innovation

Former Editor, *Crain's
Chicago Business*

Former Business Editor,
Chicago Sun-Times

Fun Fact:

Dan Miller was the
founding editor of
Crain's Chicago Business,
and was formerly the
business editor for the
Chicago Sun-Times. Dan
was inducted into the
Chicago Journalism Hall
of Fame in 2005.

David was an early civic leader who helped Chicago entrepreneurs access the resources they needed to scale. Together, Michael and David were among the earlier civic leaders who focused intently on Chicago entrepreneurs.

Linked to David Weinstein was **Jerry Roper**, President and CEO of the Chicagoland Chamber of Commerce from 1993 to 2013, which housed the CEC in its formative years. "For more than twenty years, Jerry was a tireless advocate and a tremendous partner for strengthening Chicago's business climate and ensuring a stronger economic future for our city," former Chicago Mayor Rahm Emanuel said in a statement following Jerry's passing in 2015. "Jerry understood that entrepreneurs and small businesses form the backbone of a vibrant and growing economy for Chicagoland. His work was essential, and his contributions to our economic vibrancy will be long lasting." Many of Chicago's most prolific entrepreneurs and leaders recall the foundational role that Jerry played before Chicago's innovation ecosystem became the juggernaut that it is today. Jerry was "a great ambassador for the city," serial entrepreneur Howard Tullman said following Jerry's retirement.

Another pioneering organization was the Chicago Innovation Awards. Founded in 2002, it is the region's largest annual celebration of new products, services, and businesses. Now known as Chicago Innovation, the organization has been a pillar of the innovation community, working to "recognize, celebrate, convene, and connect" notes Matt McCall, Partner at Pritzker Group Venture Capital. The life forces behind the formation of the organization were **Tom Kuczmarski**, President of innovation consulting firm Kuczmarski Innovation and professor of innovation at Northwestern's Kellogg School of Management since 1980, and **Dan Miller**, former Business Editor of the *Chicago Sun-Times* and former Editor of *Crain's Chicago Business*. "By creating an awards program for Chicago innovators, Tom and Dan catalyzed the community," says Michael Krauss. "Tom is a key person in all of this," agrees Kevin Willer, Partner at Chicago Ventures. "He's been celebrating Chicago's innovators longer than anyone else and supporting it since the beginning."

In 2010, Tom and Dan were joined by **Luke Tanen**, who was hired as the organization's first Executive Director. In his first decade, Luke helped Chicago Innovation launch an array of new events and programs that have attracted a community of over thirty-thousand innovation-minded people. "The fact that Tom and Luke are still driving the innovation ecosystem today is key," says Hardik Bhatt, former Chief Information Officer for Chicago Mayor Richard Daley and Illinois Governor Bruce Rauner. "We have consistent leaders who have stayed here to focus on taking Chicago to the next level."

The Illinois Technology Association is seen by many as another stalwart of Chicago's technology ecosystem, founded in 2005 by **Fred Hoch** and **Terry Howerton**. By squarely focusing on supporting the growth of mid-size business-to-business technology companies, Fred and Terry have zeroed in on advancing the backbone of Chicago's technology sector prowess.

Following in the footsteps of the CEC, Chicago Innovation, and the Illinois Technology Association, another group called Built In Chicago came on the scene in 2011. Founded by Chicago technology entrepreneur **Matt Moog**, Built In Chicago started as a social network and blogging platform rooted in a love of Chicago, its people and tech. Early on, Matt brought in Co-founders **Maria Katris**, CEO, and **Adam Calica**, VP of Product and Growth, and together they acted as evangelists during the years when Chicago's innovation ecosystem experienced an uptick in activity.

During this same time period, 1871 was founded by the Chicagoland Entrepreneurial Center. The incubator was financed primarily by venture capitalist J.B. Pritzker and an economic development grant from the State of Illinois. **Kevin Willer**, who co-opened the Google Chicago office in the early 2000s, was an important choice as 1871's first CEO. Kevin had been instrumental in growing Google's Chicago presence from two employees to over five hundred. As Google's Chicago office grew, so did Kevin's role as an advocate for entrepreneurship in Chicago. Kevin was tasked with making 1871 the go-to incubator and coworking hub for digital technology startups in Chicago. To this day, Kevin is one of the most vocal cheerleaders for digital tech entrepreneurship, and a frequently seen speaker at events focused on telling the stories of Chicago's innovators.

The incubator received a powerful adrenaline shot in the arm when its leadership transitioned from Kevin Willer to **Howard Tullman**, who has worked tirelessly to galvanize Chicago's startup scene for decades. At 1871, Howard turbo-charged efforts to support the growth of Chicago entrepreneurs. Under Howard's leadership, 1871 became the number one ranked university-affiliated business incubator in the country. It's a fact that Howard is proud to talk about, which he does at many events and interviews as a spokesperson for Chicago tech. In 2018, Howard became the Executive Director of the Ed Kaplan Family Institute for Innovation and Tech Entrepreneurship at Illinois Tech, helping to create the next generation of technology leaders. Howard knows exactly what it takes to be that kind of leader. Over the last fifty years, he has successfully founded more than a dozen high-tech companies, and he continues to invest and mentor countless entrepreneurs.

Troy Henikoff is another serial entrepreneur in Chicago who used his talents to help the next generation of Chicago startup leaders by taking the helm at Techstars Chicago, a nationally recognized three-month boot camp for startups. "I think Troy did a huge amount with Techstars and bringing that to the Chicago startup ecosystem," says Linda Darragh, who oversees entrepreneurship education at Northwestern's Kellogg School of Management. "Troy's hand has been in a lot of things over time. He's done a lot." Some of Troy's other notable efforts in Chicago include launching and selling SurePayroll for $115 million in 2011, and starting venture capital firm MATH Venture Partners along with tech entrepreneur **Mark Achler**.

While recognizing community connectors and cheerleaders, it's worth pointing out again that Chicago is at the forefront of embracing female-founded companies. A September 2018 *Inc. Magazine* article noted that Chicago "boasts the greatest concentration of women founders in the nation." To understand how Chicago came to deserve this accolade, one must take note of **Hedy Ratner**, Co-founder and President Emeritus of the

Women's Business Development Center, the largest, oldest, and most comprehensive women's business assistance center in the U.S. An advocate and activist for women's issues for more than forty years, Hedy has dedicated her life to social justice and advocacy for the empowerment of women across the world. Since launching the Women's Business Development Center in Chicago in 1986, Hedy and her organization have served over eighty-five thousand women in the Midwest on their journeys to starting and growing their own companies. The landscape of Chicago female entrepreneurship would not be the same without Hedy.

There are many other individuals in the Chicago region who have made a significant impact as community connectors and cheerleaders – people who head up the region's network of incubators, coworking spaces, business membership organizations, and so forth. While each one truly deserves his or her own paragraph, if not full page, it is time to revert attention toward a unique set of innovation-minded leaders who ascended to the highest levels of government in Chicago and Illinois. In doing so, they brought the public sector to the forefront of the story that details Chicago's rise as a global innovation hub.

Public Sector Performers

An inflection point in Chicago's tech and entrepreneurial journey occurred around 2010 and 2011. These are the years when the rate of innovation activity started to accelerate. It is not a coincidence that 2011 is also the year that **Rahm Emanuel** took the reins as Mayor of Chicago.

As a candidate, Mayor Emanuel understood technology's capacity to affect change. "The

Brenna Berman

CEO, City Tech Collaborative

Former Chief Information Officer, City of Chicago –Department of Innovation & Technology

Favorite Innovation:

The RideSafer Vest

"Usually you put the car seat in the car. The RideSafer Vest puts the car seat on the kid so you can put the kid in the car. It is the answer to how I can leverage ride-shares with two kids."

Fun Fact:

As Chief Information Officer and Commissioner of the Department of Innovation and Technology under Mayor Rahm Emanuel, Brenna was key in leading the city's first-ever tech plan that placed special emphasis on making Chicago a leading "smart city."

Mayor campaigned on tech-focused commitments around the values of open data, transparency, and governing more effectively through technology," says Brenna Berman, a leader at IBM who became the City of Chicago's Chief Information Officer in 2011.

Mayor Emanuel's background as a business-savvy investor and political veteran who spent many years in the White House serving under Presidents Bill Clinton and Barack Obama enabled him to become an incredibly effective mayor. His ability to leverage his global network of power brokers coupled with the tight-knit bond he kept with Chicago's entrepreneurial leaders helped Mayor Emanuel deliver the resources that innovators needed to succeed. So much so, in fact, that according to an April 2019 *Chicago Magazine* article, during Rahm's tenure "the share of the city's economy attributed to tech more than quadrupled."

"Being the mayor of Chicago is a global job," notes Howard Tullman. "It's important to attract talent. It's important to get financing, investment, and connections." Mayor Emanuel did it all.

"Rahm was the forward-looking mayor that we needed," remarks Kevin Willer. "He has been a great friend to the entrepreneurial and tech community in Chicago. He had a global network of people to bring to our city. He can get Elon Musk. He can get Sheryl Sandberg."

Mayor Emanuel was truly Chicago's chief marketing officer, acting as the city's top ambassador as he regularly promoted the virtues of conducting business in Chicago. "We traveled across the world with him," continues Kevin, who often accompanied the Mayor and other entrepreneurial leaders during his trips to build partnerships around the globe. A visit to Israel in 2017 focused on cross-country collaboration utilizing new clean water technologies is one such example.

No one was better than Mayor Emanuel when it came to promoting Chicago's story to the rest of the world. Take this excerpt from a speech the Mayor gave in 2017 to woo a large corporate headquarters to Chicago:

> *"They're looking for world-class talent and world-class institutions of higher learning, they're looking for a world-class aviation system, a world-class public transportation system, and a city that's affordable for their workforce to live in and not live two and a half hours away by car. By every measure, Chicago is at the top."*

Mayor Emanuel's drive to bring outside corporations into Chicago gave the city a number one ranking in corporate relocation for six years in a row, according to *Site Selection Magazine*.

As reported in the aforementioned April 2019 *Chicago Magazine* article, "Salesforce, Facebook, Yelp, and Google all opened Chicago offices while Emanuel was mayor. When Google was planning to open a Midwestern headquarters in the Fulton Market district, Emanuel 'was in almost constant communication with their executives,' said Andrea Zopp, a former deputy mayor who became president and CEO of World Business Chicago. 'I think if you talk to any CEO who's moved here, they'll tell you he's relentless.'"

When he wasn't recruiting companies to come to Chicago, he was laser-focused on what Chicago's current crop of innovative companies needed. "Rahm was so collaborative and supportive of entrepreneurship," says Andrea Zopp. He listened intently to the needs of entrepreneurs to better understand how his office could partner in their success. The mayor's annual brown bag luncheon with the twenty-five winners of the Chicago Innovation Awards, which he did every year while he was in office, is indicative of his closeness to Chicago's entrepreneurs. He was a frequent attendee at ribbon cuttings when a Chicago startup reached a milestone, such as surpassing two hundred employees or opening a new office.

Mayor Emanuel was able to find success in the ecosystem because he espoused the values of the C.H.I.C.A.G.O. Way. "During a time when political divisiveness was at a peak, Mayor Emanuel made it clear to everyone in the country that Chicago is a city that welcomes anyone," details Andrea Zopp. "He will stand up and fight for you. He's very moral. In a world where we have a gross absence of moral leadership, we had a leader who felt very strongly about right and wrong. He was clear about holding himself accountable and doing things that weren't always politically popular. But they were the right things to do. And he held me and everyone else accountable for doing the right things too."

Of course, Mayor Emanuel wasn't the only public sector leader who accelerated Chicago's rise as an innovation capital. Before Mayor Emanuel, there was Mayor **Richard M. Daley**, who presided over Chicago from 1989 to 2011. Richard Daley's tenure as mayor was marked by great investments in Chicago's infrastructure, especially a series of mega projects along Chicago's lakefront. This included tearing up Meigs Field Airport to construct the 91-acre waterfront park out of Northerly Island, funding the construction of 25-acre Millennium Park in the heart of downtown, several expansions of the McCormick Place convention center, and a significant reconstruction of Navy Pier to transform it into one of the city's most popular tourist destinations.

These projects, among many others undertaken during Mayor Daley's reign, enhanced the overall quality of life for Chicagoans living and working in the city center. The business community grew, and by the turn of the century, business leaders began embracing technology more than they had in the past. The concept of an "innovation ecosystem" was still a very nascent idea at the time.

While Mayor Daley was not a technologist himself, he understood the value of convening technology leaders to discuss ways to improve the condition of the city and its residents. The MCTA was created thanks to the support of Mayor Daley. "Rich Daley deserves a lot of credit for the success of the MCTA," notes the Council's former leader, Michael Krauss. "Daley gave us his blessing and his brand. That was important. He was genuine about wanting to see us make Chicago a better place by lending a hand to the technology community."

Years before the dotcom boom took hold of the city, Mayor Daley brought resources together to ensure that Chicago would improve its readiness for technology entrepreneurs. The City's Technology Development Initiative provided $70 million in financial incentives to build technology infrastructure and development projects, including the financing of two important tech centers in Chicago. One was the Lakeside Technology Center, and the other was 600 W. Chicago. Formerly the headquarters of mail order and department store retailer Montgomery Ward, 600 W. Chicago transformed into one of the most significant tech centers in Chicago, home to companies like Groupon, Uptake, Echo Global Logistics, and others.

In addition to mayors, there have been governors who played key roles in the development of Chicago's innovation community as well. Governor **Pat Quinn** is one example who attached the resources of the state with the needs of innovators and entrepreneurs. The launch of 1871, the crown jewel of Chicago's network of entrepreneurship incubators, was perhaps the most significant contribution made by the State of Illinois to the tech ecosystem under Governor Quinn's leadership. Governor Quinn provided $2.3 million of state funding to build 1871's initial fifty thousand square foot space. After seeing how powerful an impact 1871 was having on the city, Governor Quinn doubled down and invested an additional $2.5 million several years later to expand 1871's physical space by 50 percent, enabling it to house alumni companies, venture capital firms, and several incubators, accelerators and other programs for entrepreneurs.

While the central business district was flourishing during the 2000s and 2010s, there was one government leader who took a slightly more regional approach to economic development. To create a truly inclusive economic hub of activity, one must be focused on all members of the workforce. Cook County President **Toni Preckwinkle** made it a special focus to always extend a welcoming hand to segments of the population that often went unnoticed and under supported, especially people living in Chicago's south and west suburbs. A good example of President Preckwinkle's commitment to preparing people with the skills they need to succeed is The Chicago Cook Workforce Partnership, which she created in 2012. As noted on the Cook County website:

> *"The Chicago Cook Workforce Partnership combines federal and philanthropic resources to broaden the reach and impact of workforce development services for both employers and job seekers. As the largest nonprofit workforce development system in the nation, the Partnership has helped place more than 60,000 individuals in employment, collaborated with more than 2,000 employers and administers more than $300 million in federal and philanthropic funds. The Partnership's network of more than 50 community-based organizations, 10 American Job Centers, and sector-driven workforce centers serve 132 municipalities."*

It's this scale of impact that has driven Toni Preckwinkle to become a very effective leader. Moreover, as a former teacher herself, she knows the value of teaching new skills to the masses.

Andrea Zopp is an example of someone who has been a champion for Chicago's neighborhoods for her entire career. She is currently the CEO of World Business Chicago, and works to bring foreign direct investment and corporate relocations to the city, as well as lead efforts to elevate the region as a participant in the global conversation. Prior to this, Andrea was the CEO of the Chicago Urban League, until she was later appointed as Rahm Emanuel's Deputy Mayor and Chief Neighborhood Development Officer. At the time of the appointment, then Mayor Emanuel said, "I know she has the credentials, the credibility, and the commitment to our communities to deliver on the mission of building safer and stronger neighborhoods from the inside out."

At the time of this writing, Chicago Mayor **Lori Lightfoot** and Illinois Governor J.B. Pritzker are both in the beginning of their terms. It's too early to fully measure how the City and State will further impact Chicago's innovators under their respective leadership. However, it is very encouraging to see the directions that Mayor Lightfoot and Governor Pritzker are heading. They've taken a very inclusive approach to stimulating innovation and business development.

For example, in October of 2019 Mayor Lightfoot announced a new initiative called "INVEST South/West" aimed at revitalizing ten historically underdeveloped neighborhoods in the south and west sides of the city. In doing so, she also focused on galvanizing the corporate community to lend a hand. Time will tell how significantly this initiative will impact these regions, but the need to boost economic development in those neighborhoods is high, and the mayor's determination is strong.

As for Governor Pritzker, his track record of supporting innovators spans decades. He joins several individuals who have had a hugely outsized role as investors who have partnered with Chicago entrepreneurs to make a significant impact.

The Financiers

Chicago has many venture capital firms and angel investor groups that have looked locally to give homegrown entrepreneurs their first big check. Lightbank, Chicago Ventures, Origin Ventures, MK Capital, OCA Ventures, Sandbox Industries, Apex Venture Partners, FireStarter Fund, Corazon Capital, MATH Venture Partners, Jumpstart Ventures, Hyde Park Angels, and Wildcat Angels are among the legion of firms that have welcomed Chicago entrepreneurs with the opportunity to fundraise. But one firm that stands out among them is Pritzker Group Venture Capital, one of the city's most active venture capital firms, especially in deals that involve later stage growth. Since its founding in 1996, the person instrumental to the firm's success and a major change-maker in Chicago is **J.B. Pritzker**.

Though he was described as "Chicago's business venture capitalist" by *Crain's Chicago Business*, labeling J.B. Pritzker as an investor does not fully appreciate his role in this story. J.B. is a connector, a community builder, and a champion of innovators and entrepreneurs. "J.B. brought together his peers to think about how we can make Chicago a top producer of entrepreneurs. He knew what elements were needed to create a thriving ecosystem," shares Holly Copeland, who previously oversaw innovation for Illinois Governor Pat Quinn before becoming Senior Director of Public Affairs and Corporate Social Responsibility for pharmaceutical company Horizon Therapeutics.

It's J.B.'s leadership that gave way to him being elected the 43rd Governor of Illinois in 2018. But long before J.B. held political office, his focus was on investing in great companies and helping to build organizations that would sustain entrepreneurship for years to come.

Among J.B.'s most well-known efforts in the Chicago entrepreneurial community is the creation of 1871. "This place wouldn't have happened without J.B.," asserts 1871's first CEO Kevin Willer. J.B. is also credited with helping start the CEC, the Illinois Venture Capital Association, and having major influence in launching healthcare incubator MATTER, physical product manufacturing center mHUB, online technology community Built In Chicago, and other innovation-centric organizations like Techstars Chicago and Chicago Ventures.

Jim O'Connor Jr., the Global Head of Venture Capital for William Blair and former Chairman of the CEC, is another Chicago financier who has straddled the worlds of investing and civic responsibility, much like J.B. Pritzker has so successfully done. "Jim brought a lot of venture capital to Chicago in the early days of our ecosystem's formation," says Hardik Bhatt of Amazon. "He is a consistent leader in our city."

Another local venture capital leader who helped shape the city's innovation landscape is **Nick Rosa**, who co-founded Sandbox Industries with **Bob Shapiro** in 2004. Having raised over $700 million between both Sandbox Industries and Nick's more recent venture Cultivian Sandbox, Nick has propelled Chicago to become a leader in venture investing in healthcare, food, and agriculture.

Nick doubled down on health tech when he founded the incubator Healthbox in 2012. He was also one of the co-founders of Excelerate Labs, the intensive summer accelerator for startups, which later became Techstars Chicago.

Bret Maxwell, Managing Director of MK Capital, is another stalwart in the Chicago venture capital community. He's been a decision maker in a total of nine fully invested funds, representing over $500 million in committed capital, with a special focus on bringing capital to emerging growth companies in software and cloud services. Bret is also committed to giving women more opportunities to play active roles in Chicago's startup and venture capital ecosystem. Through Bret's leadership, MK Capital became the founding sponsor of Chicago Innovation's Women Mentoring Co-op, an initiative launched in 2015 that is aimed at empowering, connecting, and propelling female innovators in the Chicago region.

For years, **Matt McCall**, Partner at Pritzker Group Venture Capital, has been a voice of leadership among Chicago's venture capitalists. Matt has invested in over seventy companies, completed more than four hundred financings, and looked at over twenty thousand business plans across three boom/bust cycles. A consummate thought provoker via his blog, "Something Ventured" (formerly "VC Confidential"), and a frequent speaker at events, Matt is an avid researcher of the historical forces that shape entrepreneurial success, and often talks about the importance of "changing the narrative" in order to re-position Chicago's standing as a global hub of innovation.

Origin Ventures is another prominent Chicago-area venture capital firm that has enjoyed well-earned success; for example, they were the first institutional investor in Grubhub. At the helm since its founding in 1999 have been **Steve Miller** and **Bruce Barron**. Steve and Bruce understand the importance of perpetuating the cycle of entrepreneurship and, in fact, have given $5 million to their alma mater, the University of Illinois, to bring entrepreneurial education to Illinois students.

While there are many other venture capitalists in the Chicago region, each with its own area of expertise, there is one category of investor that merits an extra spotlight: the angel investor. There are several angel investor groups in Chicago, like Hyde Park Angels, which convenes people who are looking to deploy capital to startups. But there are also individuals who seek out and support Chicago startups on their own. One of the most active of these angel investors over the past two decades is **Mike Gamson**, who formerly led LinkedIn's Chicago office before becoming CEO of legal technology firm Relativity in 2019.

Amanda Lannert, CEO of Jellyvision, thinks back to Mike's influence on the earlier days of the ecosystem: "There's not a big deal that I ran into that Mike Gamson hadn't seeded with a big check; he was everywhere. I call him 'the patron saint' for that reason, he was just giving out money all over the place, and would seed all of these companies all by himself." Serial entrepreneur Sam Yagan continues, "I'm sure Mike is overexposed to Chicago startups in his portfolio, but he's decided that this is how he's going to help. His goal is to make money, but my guess is that if he went to a financial advisor, they'd say to diversify his money into other cities."

Mike is an example of the type of investor who looks at investing differently. He does it in a holistic way, recognizing the distinct types of value he can offer. Sometimes it's money; other times it's mentorship. It's people like Mike who know the meaning behind the famous adage, "Give a man a fish, and you feed him for a day. Teach a man to fish, and you feed him for a lifetime."

Talent development is at the top of Mike's personal agenda, and he views it as the critical ingredient to ensure a thriving innovation ecosystem. At an event held by the Economic Club of Chicago in January 2019 about the future of Chicago tech, Mike told the crowd about a stat that he garnered from LinkedIn: "Computer science grads from schools in Illinois are 4.5 times more likely to work in Chicago at some point during their careers than any other city." When he said this, one could feel the energy in the room shift. The future was brimming with possibility. That's

Amanda Lannert

CEO, Jellyvision

Favorite Innovation:

Genome mapping

"My father-in-law was diagnosed with Hodgkin's Lymphoma thirteen years ago, and what science is doing now to fight cancer is unbelievable. We are changing the narrative of what it means to have a cancer diagnosis."

Fun Fact:

Amanda won the prestigious CEO of the Year award at Built In Chicago's 2014 Moxie Awards. Her company, Jellyvision, is a regular on "Best Place to Work" lists.

why people at the forefront of shaping talent over the years have been so impactful in driving the Chicago innovation ecosystem forward.

The Talent Shapers

If knowledge is power, then Chicago is indeed a powerhouse. Outside of Boston, Chicago is the only city in the country to boast two business schools that are annually ranked top five in the nation: Northwestern's Kellogg School of Management and the University of Chicago's Booth School of Business. Behind these schools lay an array of others that churn out talent on a yearly basis. DePaul University, University of Illinois, Illinois Institute of Technology, Loyola University, the School of the Art Institute Chicago, and dozens of other universities collectively have made Chicago one of the nation's best-educated big cities. According to the 2017 American Community Survey, Chicago has more people over age twenty-five with a bachelor's degree or higher than any of the country's four other largest cities.

The educational system in Chicago is a massive operation. Thousands upon thousands of educators have each left their thumbprint on the lives of talented young people who have been trained in Chicago's schools. What lies ahead is a selection of people who, as Sam Yagan said at the outset of this chapter, "played outsized roles," especially as it relates to entrepreneurship education at the university level. This includes a pair of women who have been credited with running the entrepreneurship departments at two of the best business schools in the world, along with a handful of entrepreneurs-turned-philanthropists who chose to invest their charitable dollars into a worthy cause: the future minds of America.

A healthy rivalry exists between Northwestern's Kellogg School of Management and the University of Chicago Booth School of Business. The friendly competition pushes each school to outdo the other in its student offerings and fundraising activities. One person who has the rare experience of playing on both teams is **Linda Darragh**, who has headed up the entrepreneurship departments for each of these schools at different points in time over the past two decades.

Starting out in 1998, Linda taught Entrepreneurship and New Venture Formulation at Kellogg. From there, she was plucked by the South Side rival to head up its entrepreneurship department, which she led from 2005 to 2012, only to then go back to Kellogg where she has overseen the Levy Institute for Entrepreneurial Practice ever since. Where Linda goes, there is a wake of entrepreneurship that follows. According to statistics published in 2019 by Northwestern's Kellogg School of Management, 73 percent of students are enrolled in an entrepreneurship course. The school now offers over sixty entrepreneurship-related courses, marking an explosion of new offerings from just a decade ago, along with thirty clubs and organizations supporting entrepreneurship.

At the 2018 Momentum Awards, the annual fundraiser for Chicago's leading digital tech incubator 1871, two pioneers of entrepreneurship education in Chicago were honored. One was Linda Darragh. The other was **Ellen Rudnick**, who served as the Executive Director of the Polsky Center for Entrepreneurship at the University of Chicago Booth School of Business from 1999-2016. Alongside Professor **Steven Kaplan** who is also credited with helping to launch the school's entrepreneurship program, Ellen helped Booth become a global leader in entrepreneurship education.

Perhaps one of the best proof points is Booth's New Venture Challenge, an annual competition that fetes student entrepreneurs with prize money. In 2015, the New Venture Challenge was ranked the #1 university accelerator program in the nation according to the Seed Accelerator Rankings Program. Companies like Braintree, which was later acquired by PayPal for $850 million, and Grubhub, which went public in 2014, are among a notable list of student-run companies that won this prestigious business plan competition. When the New Venture Challenge celebrated its twentieth birthday in 2016, it had already seen 800 startups pitch on its stage, roughly 140 of which are still in business. Those companies have gone on to raise more than $400 million in investments, and generated $3 billion in exits, as reported in a 2016 *Chicago Tribune* article. If it weren't for Ellen's decades of commitment to U of C student entrepreneurs, none of the groundwork would have been laid for these types of results.

Offering world-class entrepreneurship programming isn't cheap. It comes with a hefty price tag. Funds are needed to not only attract the nation's leading academicians, but also to equip students and faculty with cutting-edge technology, labs, and the physical space for learning to occur. Thankfully, Chicago is home to some entrepreneurs-turned-philanthropists who have dedicated significant dollars to ensuring that local university entrepreneurship programming is top notch.

Larry Levy is a longtime benefactor to entrepreneurship at Northwestern University's Kellogg School of Management. He knows a thing or two about being an entrepreneur. Started in 1978 as a single delicatessen in Chicago, Larry built Levy Restaurants into a food service empire, consisting of restaurants and one of the largest sports concession businesses in the country. "Larry has been a life long entrepreneur known for his successful business ventures, and as he will admit, has learned many tough lessons about entrepreneurship along the way," says Linda Darragh. "Larry generously and continually imparts his knowledge to newly minted as well as scaling entrepreneurs. This passion for entrepreneurship launched and continues to guide the impact of the Larry and Carol Levy Institute for Entrepreneurial Practice at Kellogg."

Across town, the Polsky Center for Entrepreneurship at the University of Chicago's Booth School of Business gets its namesake from **Michael Polsky**, CEO of Chicago-based clean energy company Invenergy. After starting with a single wind farm in Tennessee, Michael built Invenergy into a billion-dollar clean energy company. "Polsky provides yet another example of the extraordinary entrepreneurial energy that immigrants bring to the U.S., and of what they can get out of it," noted David Whitford in a 2017 *Inc. Magazine* article. He also never lost sight of supporting other entrepreneurs. Michael single-handedly accelerated the entrepreneurship prowess of the Booth School, bestowing $50 million to fuel the Polsky Center. "The Polsky Center's expansion is designed to make it easier for entrepreneurs to get their ideas to market and connect with the necessary resources along the way," says John Flavin, former head of the Polsky Center.

Another entrepreneur-turned-philanthropist that has changed the talent development landscape in Chicago is **Joe Mansueto**, Founder of global financial services firm Morningstar. Joe was the first Chicagoan to sign the Giving Pledge, an initiative started by Bill Gates and Warren Buffet to secure the commitment of the world's wealthiest families to give away at least half of their fortunes to philanthropic causes. Joe supports many causes, but one area of giving that is near and dear to his heart is education.

Through his foundation, Joe has funneled $60 million to the University of Chicago to build a world-class library and the Mansueto Institute for Urban Innovation, designed to train students to become future urban scholars and leaders.

Shifting attention towards another university on the rise, the Illinois Institute of Technology has become a magnet for both local and international students looking to advance their skills. One of the leading funders of talent development there is **Ed Kaplan**, Founder of Zebra Technologies, one of the world's leading manufacturers of marking, tracking, and computer printing technologies. "Chicago has a lot of technology luminaries," explains Michael Krauss. "Ed Kaplan is one of them, and deserves a lot of credit in the story about Chicago as a center of technology." In 2018, Ed gave $11 million to launch the Ed Kaplan Family Institute for Innovation and Tech Entrepreneurship at Illinois Institute of Technology. The focus of the Kaplan Institute is on transforming key parts of the university's curricula, with an emphasis on applied creativity, collaboration, and hands-on experiential learning.

To say that talent shapers are resigned to only the university setting would be short sighted. There are many workforce development organizations in Chicago committed to upskilling people, especially those who have the hardest time affording the expense of a college degree.

An exemplary organization in this field is i.c.stars, a nonprofit co-founded in 1999 by **Sandee Kastrul** aimed at identifying, training, and jump-starting technology careers for Chicago-area low-income young adults. These young adults, who have traditionally lacked access to education and employment, have thrived in i.c.stars programming, demonstrating extraordinary potential for success in the business world and for impact in their communities. i.c.stars participants take part in a four-month boot camp, consisting of twelve-hours-per-day, project-based learning in which they develop software solutions for large corporations, followed by a two-year residency that offers continuing education, mentoring, job placement, and networking activities. The biggest winners are the low-income adults. The i.c.stars participants who graduate from Sandee's program see a three hundred percent increase in their average annual income. Employers are clearly willing to pay a premium for the unique talents these adults now possess.

Bringing the People Together

As mentioned at the outset of this discussion, the people highlighted here cannot take all the credit for Chicago's climb as a city of innovation. There are countless other entrepreneurs, community builders, government officials, investors, professors, corporate leaders, and philanthropists who have left lasting impressions on the Chicago innovation community. But there is no question that Chicago would not be where it is today without the people profiled in this chapter. They indeed played outsized roles that forever changed the Chicago narrative.

There is a common thread between many of these individuals; they have gone above and beyond to source and distribute talent and resources. These two elements are the lifeblood of a business ecosystem, and the ease through which they flow between individuals, organizations, and industries plays a massive role in the region's ability to compete on a global scale.

CHAPTER
7
BALANCING HUMAN AND FINANCIAL CAPITAL

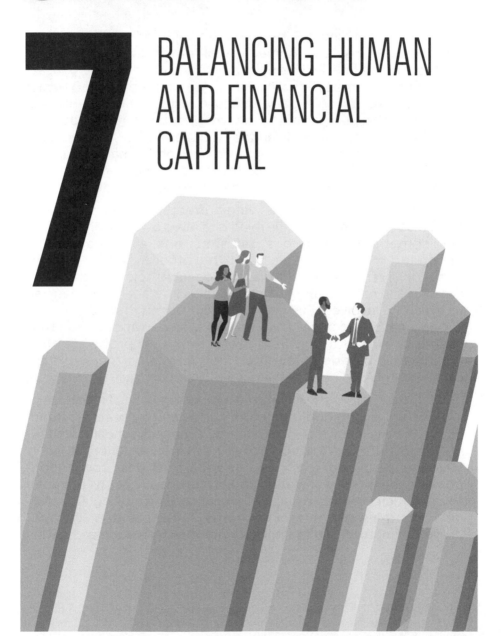

CHAPTER 7: BALANCING HUMAN AND FINANCIAL CAPITAL

Early each morning in Sub-Saharan Africa, a red-billed oxpecker rustles awake inside its home: a small patch of discarded hair nestled within a hole in the side of a tree. At just under two ounces in weight, the small bird grooms its grey feathers and quickly takes off in search of its daily roost. Amidst the drought-ridden, predator-laden plains, it has found a regular perch free of danger and plentiful in resources. It lands as it does each day on the back of a grazing rhinoceros and begins to peck at the many ticks and insects that have accumulated on the large animal's hard-to-reach backside, a welcome respite for the inflexible pachyderm.

In exchange for acting as a living buffet table and warding off otherwise eager predators, the rhino is relieved of its uncomfortable and sometimes dangerous parasites, and even warned of oncoming threats by calls from the other small birds that occasionally fly overhead. It is a textbook example of mutualistic symbiosis in nature; intimate interspecies interactions beneficial to everyone involved. Each party carries a strength or capability in one area, be it dexterity or size, and a need in another – in this case a lack of resources and protection, or a propensity for unreachable parasites. Together, they form a partnership that serves to improve both of their lives.

While relatively rare in nature, the mutually beneficial relationship is prevalent among business communities, and a key cornerstone of the Chicago innovation ecosystem. In a melting pot of industries, sectors, institutions, and companies both for and nonprofit, all of which range in size and tenure, there are limitless connection points to be made where individuals and organizations are able to offer their plentiful resources in exchange for filling a gap or need. As the most diverse economy in the country, Chicago provides a natural habitat for this kind of cross-sector exchange.

Defining the Pillars

Unlike many other cities that specialize in a particular industry (e.g. technology in San Francisco, finance in New York, manufacturing in Detroit), Chicago's strength lies in its diversity. And innovation permeates each of these industries as well. As Hardik Bhatt, former State CIO explains, "One key thing I have seen is how the innovation ecosystem is as diverse as the industry base. We have consumer tech, gov tech, bio tech, fintech, and more." To this point in the discussion, there has been ample explanation into the values that guide the manner in which the innovation ecosystem collaborates, but less in terms of how it actually happens.

In order to fully appreciate the intricate ways through which the constituents within the Chicago innovation ecosystem interact, it is important to dissect the pieces and appreciate what each element contributes to the overall community, as well as what it requires in return to thrive. These pieces, or pillars, are defined in no particular order of importance as: **Startups, Large Corporations, Financial Institutions, Nonprofits, Civic Organizations, Incubators and Universities.**

The pathways through which these entities interact are widespread and diverse, each with auxiliary partners playing secondary and tertiary roles. Together, they create a web-like infrastructure that forms the foundation of the Chicago innovation ecosystem. If one were to dissect this collaborative bedrock into its major distinguishable parts, they would see each individual partnership and transaction as a two-sided give and take. One party offers something they have in excess in exchange for something they lack, such that each is left in a better position than where they started. This is the true essence of the mutually beneficial relationship; a capital balance.

The Capital Balance: Human and Financial

While altruism is one of the values espoused by the Chicago innovation ecosystem, it would be disingenuous, and frankly naïve, to make the assertion that key business decisions are made selflessly. Collaboration among entities is not an act of charity, but rather a calculated transaction in which both parties are offering their resources to one another in exchange for the solution

Matt McCall

Partner, Pritzker Group
Venture Capital

Fun Fact:

Matt has invested in over
70 companies, completed
over 400 financings, and
reviewed over 20,000
business plans.

to a need. It is a balance between what one carries in excess, what one lacks, and how their neighbor complements those internal needs.

The notion of looking to others to mutually solve problems is inherently Chicagoan, and is a crucial element to the success of the ecosystem. "The thing that would destroy this ecosystem would be a loss in that sense of community," says Matt McCall, Partner at Pritzker Group Venture Capital. In picturing a Chicago without collaboration, Matt continues, "If everyone starts self-optimizing, all the oil in the engine dries up. What would happen to recruiting? Raising money? Customer introductions? If all of that stops happening and people become self-centered, and go from the scale of a community to a series of small individual entities, everything gets blown off the table." Wherever possible, innovators in the region tend to have a unique affinity to find those complementary partnerships in a variety of forms.

This balance is maintained between two distinct forms of capital that fuel organizations of all types. Be they large or small, old or new, for-profit, nonprofit, or governmental, the two critical resources that drive organizational viability are human and financial capital. The two are interrelated and deeply depend on one another, but few organizations have an excess of both. Many are proficient in one but profoundly lacking in the other. There are entire industries that are devoted to cultivating capital, be it human or financial, and solely serve to seek out partnerships with under-performing or ill-equipped organizations that could use a boost.

When taken at a bird's-eye view, the cultivation and distribution of human and financial capital creates an infrastructure through which the different industries and sectors interact. It is a balance between the "haves" and the "have nots," but almost impossibly results in a net positive for all involved. The ways in which these two forms of capital interact are intricate and varied, but it's important to have a basic understanding of their composition before delving into the details.

Financial Capital

The more obvious of the two, financial capital, refers to money. It is what allows organizations to build, produce, manufacture, and distribute products and services to their customers. They use it to expand geographically, advertise en masse, and develop cutting-edge technologies. It can be used to hire talented professionals, incentivize and motivate employees, appease shareholders, and invest in prospective projects or organizations.

Organizations that are plentiful in financial capital tend to be large corporations, venture capital firms, banks and other financial institutions, and several government entities. They are capable of making large investments into their own growth, as well as the growth of others. But why would an institution give away such a valuable resource as its financial capital? In many cases, it is to subsidize their primary limiting factor: a deficiency in human capital.

Human Capital

Though seldom included on the balance sheet, human capital is an all-too-often overlooked asset that is vital to every organization. Human capital is a measure of the skills, education, capacity, and attributes of people that influence the productive capacity and earning potential of an organization. It is something that no company can live without, regardless of industry, sector, or size.

Human capital encompasses every aspect of the talent spectrum from engineers' ability to develop groundbreaking software to the proficiency of salespeople and marketers to win new business. Examples of organizations that carry strengths in human capital are startups, universities, and incubators. It is also such a key driver for business relocation that many government agencies are purely focused on cultivating, attracting, and retaining talent in their regions.

To Kevin Willer, Partner at Chicago Ventures, the balance between human and financial capital is vital to the long-term success of the city. "The only way that the Chicago innovation ecosystem can be successful and sustainable long term is the cycle of human capital and financial capital being reinvested. Build companies, find success, exit, and then have people reinvest." There are many ways in which capital is reinvested into the community, and the diversity of interaction is what makes the nature of collaboration in Chicago so widespread and consistent.

Human Capital: The Quest for Talent

"Access to talent is key here in Chicago. We built a business centered around local talent, and imported the capital."

John Flavin, CFO, Endotronix, Inc.

Talent is such a widespread need that entire cities rally around its cultivation, attraction, and retention as a means of convincing people and organizations to relocate. As a perennial nationwide leader in corporate relocations, Chicago has made a firm push towards attracting talented engineers, entrepreneurs, and innovators. But it wasn't always a top priority; it's only within the last handful of years that the city has been claiming its stake as a top-tier source for talent.

Talent Seekers

The desperate search for talent is not unique to Chicago; it is a universal need. When Taylor Rhodes came to Chicago in 2017, he was no stranger to the woes of attracting talented engineers. As the former CEO of San Antonio-based Rackspace, a cloud-based data storage service provider, Taylor was constantly looking for ways to convince the best and brightest that his organization provided the best opportunity for them to reach their full potential. This became especially difficult as the company expanded and the need for engineers grew in tandem with increases in revenue.

In San Antonio, Taylor struggled to find talent, and put a lot of effort into searching their ecosystem to uncover where efforts were being placed to attract people. "As we evolved over time, we became bigger. We spent a lot of time thinking through the other elements of the ecosystem. We had to go to work attracting pools of capital to come to town." When Taylor found that the San Antonio ecosystem simply wasn't set up to attract talent en masse, he realized that his organization was going to have to put its money where its mouth was and invest resources into finding these engineers.

The challenges in sourcing talent loomed over Taylor's head as he transitioned to become CEO of SMS Assist, a multisite property management solutions platform. "One of the things that I was most worried about when I got here was getting great talent to consider Chicago." Little did he know that Chicago's innovation ecosystem is full of drivers, programs, organizations, and associations all geared towards that very same goal. As an outsider to the city, Taylor was surprised to see the infrastructure in place to do all of this. To him, it was just a matter of bringing people in to see everything Chicago has to offer. "If you can get them here and show them things that are going on, most people will say, 'Oh, I had no idea!'"

If You Build It, They Will Come

Taylor Rhodes isn't the only one surprised by the level of opportunity in the Chicago innovation ecosystem. As more people become aware of a region's competitive assets, they begin to come in droves. This wave of movement sends a clear message about how impactful cultivating and retaining good talent can be on a city or region; if a business can't find the right people here, they will pick up and go find it somewhere else.

At the University of Chicago, John Flavin became the head of the Polsky Center for Entrepreneurship and Innovation with the intention of helping create the place to where people and organizations would relocate. "What is happening is that you see the companies go to the talent. They are going to the talent because now for the first time the talent has the leverage. The workflow is being rewired." The game has totally changed in terms of how to approach getting the right people in the door.

For years corporations stood tall with a cementitious foundation locking them in as a safe and stable option for individuals in search of a life-long career. It was a system that held strong for decades: work hard in school to earn a degree; get a corporate gig; put in twenty to thirty years of loyal, hard work; and retire at sixty-five with a pension and a gold watch. Not anymore. The emergence of the entrepreneurial wave of opportunity, where a small group of individuals can start a company in a garage and grow to unicorn status within a few short years, has forced corporations to compete on a totally different scale.

John Flavin continues, "Companies can't just work in isolation anymore. One person can be disruptive. Now companies need to be connected at the early stage. Not because it is nice or philanthropic, but because they need to. Those large companies also don't have a monopoly on talent; they have to work double time to attract talent that is interested in impact and being a part of something new."

It's not as simple as Microsoft vs. IBM anymore. Now it's Microsoft vs. IBM vs. Facebook vs. Apple vs. Fieldglass vs. SMS Assist vs. SpotHero vs. that grad school student who is building an AI-driven marketing platform and looking for a business development VP. The opportunities exist in all trades and range in levels of security, risk, flexibility, and reward; for the first time, the onus is on corporations to work hard to convince talent that they are better than the rest. It's not enough to get bodies in the door; organizations need to find the best there is before their competition scoops them up. By literally picking up and moving to cities like Chicago, they are sending a clear message: they cannot survive without talent.

Alma Mater Matters

Right before the turn of the twentieth century, as the Spanish-American War had just broken out, the University of Chicago's School of Business was founded. Chartered as the College of Commerce and Politics, the program served as the second business-focused curriculum in the country. It wasn't until exactly one hundred years later when, in 1998, the university developed its first concentration in entrepreneurship. Thanks to a generous one-million-dollar grant from the Kauffman Foundation, the school formed what would soon become the Polsky Center for Entrepreneurship and Innovation after an additional 2002 endowment by Michael Polsky.

Housed within what is currently the top-ranked business school in the country, the Polsky Center became a flagship model for what a university could do to develop innovative and entrepreneurial talent. John Flavin describes, "Starting at Booth with the Polsky Center twenty years ago, they led the change. They were the tip of the spear for a number of years within Booth.

Programs like the New Venture Challenge got started around then, which was the number one accelerator in the country around academic, innovation, and entrepreneurship centers."

The impact that universities have on the human capital of a region is colossal. There are few better attractors of good, young talent to a city than a top-ranked university. While the University of Chicago may have had the first boots on the ground, there are a multitude of institutions across the city. As Mike Gamson describes when thinking back to his time at LinkedIn, "We did a bunch of work and understood that Chicago is the second most productive engineering graduate geography in the country." Among Booth at the U of C, Northwestern University's Kellogg School of Management, Illinois Tech's Stuart School of Business and Kaplan Institute for Innovation and Tech Entrepreneurship, Kellstadt at DePaul, Quinlan at Loyola, and more, Chicago has developed a powerhouse of business schools that bring in not only talent, but CEOs and businesses looking to snatch up valuable human capital as soon as they graduate.

As a whole, Chicago's universities have created a constant production line of human capital. Says Jai Shekhawat, Founder of Fieldglass, "We have almost the largest number of university graduates in the country within a hundred-mile radius of a big city. If you just look at Chicago, it's second behind Boston." This includes more than just programmers and engineers as well. As Mike Gamson continues, "A dirty little secret in tech is that usually only about a quarter of the jobs are technical, but the value creation is for everybody. So you can be in finance, accounting, human resources, or sales, and it

Mike Gamson

CEO, Relativity

Former SVP, Global Solutions, LinkedIn

Favorite Innovation:

The pencil

"It's simple, it works, and it has stood the test of time. And, if it breaks, you can still use it."

Fun Fact:

In addition to helping lead LinkedIn to IPO and an eventual acquisition by Microsoft, Mike has been one of Chicago's most active behind-the-scenes investors and is outspoken about his goal of boosting the size and reputation of Chicago's tech community.

can be a much more inclusive thing than people realize." In line with the diverse melting pot of industries in Chicago, the different schools bring in aspiring engineers, artists, scientists, policy makers, and more in droves.

The density, intensity, and diversity of young talent is monumentally effective on the attractiveness of a region. When Taylor Rhodes first came to Chicago, one of the things that most struck him early on was the affluence of human capital thanks to the universities. "Within two hundred miles there are many universities, and all the graduates want to move to Chicago. So, you have a very strong, young workforce, which is highly educated. I think that's a critical ingredient in innovation." These two insights get to a key component of how universities play a role in the innovation ecosystem; it's not just about cultivating human capital, but finding pathways to connect these students to local organizations and thereby retaining the talent they work so hard to develop.

Pathways to Success

Chicago isn't the only city with a laundry list of top-tier universities churning out entry- and graduate-level talent on a daily basis. Cities like Boston, Philadelphia, Toronto, and Washington D.C. also boast a multitude of legacy institutions where students develop their skills and prepare for their professional careers. What sets some regions apart from others, however, is their ability to keep that talent local once they have brought them in at the university level. It doesn't do a city much good to have the top students in the nation arrive en masse, build valuable expertise and then leave to join or start businesses elsewhere; there needs to be concrete systems in place to encourage human capital to stay local within a city's ecosystem.

Chicago's schools have taken many strides to further solidify these pathways to local success. For John Flavin, reaching outside of the university to make connections with the Chicago innovation ecosystem was an absolute necessity. "Engagement was not just about connecting faculty with outside entrepreneurs, it was also to connect with the geography we were in. We were trying to create an open, inclusive ecosystem that included the South Side as well." Strengthening pathways between university faculty and local entrepreneurs is a textbook way of helping talented students find entry points into the ecosystem, while simultaneously giving local entrepreneurs access to the human capital they crave.

Like many institutions, Polsky doesn't hide its desire to connect its students with local talent. They lead headstrong with their mission to "bridge the gap between knowledge and practice, idea and action, and research and impact through education, partnerships, and new venture creation." They literally stand on a platform for collaboration and encouragement for their students to create something for themselves, breaking into that entrepreneurial echelon of the ecosystem.

The Kaplan Institute for Innovation and Tech Entrepreneurship at Illinois Tech has a similar mission:

> The Kaplan Institute will nurture the advancement of critical and creative ideas, foster interdisciplinary and external collaboration, and create a culture that enables innovation and tech entrepreneurship to flourish on campus and throughout the larger community as well. In addition, the institute will aggressively contribute to its surroundings and to Chicago's overall economy by encouraging, supporting, and assisting its students and faculty in creating new businesses and other entrepreneurial endeavors.

For Kaplan, it's clear as day; there is a crucial need to enable students to cultivate skills so they can contribute to society in meaningful ways, and as much as possible on the local level. They share this mentality with many of the institutions in Chicago that turn their attention to the greater community as a target for guiding their graduates' future success. They do this not only because they want to help their students enter the job market, but by communicating a clear mission that their graduates will form partnerships and businesses, they can better attract high-quality candidates in the first place. John Flavin elaborates, "Universities now need to be outwardly facing because they want to do great research, plus. And the 'plus' is impact, which is a vehicle for startups to see their idea solve a problem in the outside world. Now universities need to be nimble to attract their key capital."

Universities aren't focused on their role in the local ecosystem because they are philanthropists. They run themselves like a business just like any organization, and ones that play an active part in the development of their communities understand that they can achieve mutual benefit through supplying human capital.

Without creating this supply, the ecosystem fails, and the universities fail in turn. As Flavin continues, "if you don't invest in these outward facing areas, the long-term eminence of the university is at risk. The key currency is talent – faculty and student talent."

In any given year, the Booth School of Business at the University of Chicago and Kellogg School of Management at Northwestern will each have just over one thousand students in attendance. Adding together the students from the remaining universities forms an impressive pool of talent, however a city of over 2.5 million people needs far more than a few thousand members of the workforce. While they play a key role in bringing in and cultivating talent for Chicago, local universities are not the only source of human capital in the innovation ecosystem.

From Public to Private

Human capital comes in all shapes and sizes. Diversity in race, age, gender, experience, background, and nationality plays a huge role in how successfully an organization can meet the needs of the many versus the few. These capable people range in their ability to access education through prestigious universities. Low acceptance rates accompanied with extremely high tuition result in people of less-than-elite upbringings needing to find other ways to develop their skills. This is where the local government can step in to drastically grow the local pool of human capital.

John Flavin's creed for the Polsky Center to encourage new partnerships and ventures doesn't stop with its students. There are more channels than just holding career fairs and bringing in speakers. He elaborates on governmental partnerships with universities, "We have great partnerships between the University of Chicago and other places like Chicago Public Schools and City Colleges that need to be the on-road ramps where internships are provided, demonstrating successful ventures that come out of it." He brings up a key point about these kinds of grand scale partnerships: it's important to celebrate the successes to get the word out about these programs.

It's not enough to just build the systems to encourage growth; they need to be celebrated when they prove successful. "That's something that the mayor's office and World Business Chicago work on a lot, because there's a density to tech jobs that keeps and attracts talent from the coasts," says Brenna Berman, former CIO of the city of Chicago, on building communications about Chicago's technology opportunities. The narrative needs to get out there because "it's a strong belief that we don't have tech jobs here."

There are other roles the government needs to play in attracting talent outside of university and school programs. John Flavin goes into detail about how governmental efforts need to be put towards bringing in the right kind of people: "Governments need to be able to create good talent that knows how to help build long-term economic stability, but they also need to figure out ways to keep it inside." He is right on the money; if a city or region wants to cultivate human capital, it can't just focus on growing it locally. It needs to bring it in.

One of the reasons Taylor Rhodes had so much trouble at his previous organization was a lack of human capital in the regional Texas market. With recruiting efforts running dry and frustrations at an all-time high, he recalls wanting to shout at the city government, "Hey city, smart young people don't want to live here. What are you going to do to create places they want to live, to create the amenities around the city that they would like to have in order to consider living here?" It's a simple but often unrealized concept: if the government puts investment toward making a city a place where people want to live, they will come to stay.

This goes farther than just building new roads, parks, stadiums, and sustainable infrastructure. As Hedy Ratner, Co-founder of the Women's Business Development Center, describes, "I have always looked to the government as able to provide. If you have

Hedy Ratner

Founder & President Emerita, Women's Business Development Center

Best day of my career:

"My biggest day was one of my most visible failures; when I started the Chicago Film Institute Foundation for Women. I thought I had city council support to help build it, but when I went to the council to present my case, a couple of alderman tabled it to a committee to never return to stage again. And I realized, 'well that's over, and I had better figure something else out.'"

Hedy went on to start the Women's Business Development Center, perhaps the most impactful women-focused organization in the city's history.

enough leadership that sees the importance of innovation, economic growth, inclusion, and the impact that has on society, it makes a big difference." While amenities are important for quality of life building, there are ways in which the public and private sectors can collaborate to build fruitful partnerships to encourage human capital attraction.

Human capital is a complex issue that many regions and organizations are trying to tackle. Often times, however, those that struggle the most with cultivating talent are the ones with financial capital to invest in filling those gaps.

Financial Capital

Roughly eight thousand miles east of Chicago in Sub-Saharan Africa, the oxpecker moves swiftly and evades predatory competition with relative ease. Fortunately for the bird, resources are plentiful. Rhinoceros and zebras are easy to come by, and the oxpeckers have no issue finding hosts from whom they can pluck their arthropodal appetizers. Their mutualistic relationship is built on the birds' readiness to take advantage of the resources put towards them in a way that benefits the larger creatures as well.

Not unlike this animalistic analogy, the exchange of resources between organizations in an innovation ecosystem can glean mutually beneficial results when properly applied. Financial capital is a powerful tool that goes hand in hand with human capital to develop growing organizations, and brings a return on investment to its suppliers so that they can continue the cycle.

It's About More Than Money

Financial capital is a critical resource in any business community, and its level of availability has a huge implication on the level of success of startups and smaller organizations. If universities and incubators are cultivators of human capital, venture capital firms are their financial corollary. Their amassed funds are doled out to high-opportunity organizations that can provide them with a worthwhile investment, which they use to fund future ventures. But successful venture firms are more than just glorified piggy banks; those that share the core values of the Chicago innovation ecosystem understand that their capital input comes with significant fiduciary responsibility as well.

Long before SMS Assist breached the one billion-dollar valuation to become a unicorn, then-CFO Marc Shiffman was one of a select few on the chief team in search of funding. He was looking for more than just money, however, and finding the right source for that capital was a challenge in and of itself. Now the CEO of the organization, Marc recalls, "In the early years, getting the right person to fund you was critical to your success. And it's not just the green, it's not just the money. It's the people who are going to come with the money. We wanted more than your check." To Marc and the SMS Assist team, the money was just one piece of the puzzle.

The additional value add from venture firms is their ability to provide not only a source of cash flow, but connections, council, support, and other resources that help an organization grow effectively. This is the true essence of financial capital, and it is what sets apart thriving venture and private capital firms from one-and-done seed funds. Marc elaborates on what he was looking for from potential funders that made the task of deciding on the correct firm so difficult:

> "We realized that you could raise money from anyone anywhere, but what was going to be your contribution to help us become what we hoped SMS would be one day? How do we achieve our goal through you and your support? Not by dropping your name because you're a high-net-worth person, but are you going to make an introduction for us on the retail side? Are you going to bring customers in? Are you going to help with our technology build out? Are you going to make introductions to other people who could potentially invest?"

Not everyone is able to be as selective as the SMS Assist team in terms of where they get their millions of investment dollars from. For most Midwestern entrepreneurs, it is a grueling task to scrounge together funds to take their company from Series A to B and beyond. This is where Chicago's value of "calculated risk-taking" really comes into play, for better or worse for hungry entrepreneurs. Mike Gamson goes into detail about Chicago's culture and breakdown of venture investments: "We have a rich tapestry of seed-level funding, and a reasonable set of options at the A-level. When you start talking about people writing B and beyond sized checks (i.e. greater than $10 million), there are fewer players, and they are on the very conservative side." Whether they are considering an investment in a group with a great story behind a product entering a crowded market, or an engineer with a groundbreaking technology with unclear application, venture firms in Chicago aren't always keen to sign on the dotted line unless they see real, actionable potential.

Coming off a multi-billion dollar exit from the sale of his vendor management software company, Fieldglass, Jai Shekhawat understood better than most what it takes from a financial capital perspective to grow an organization. But back in 1999 when he was just breaking ground on his company, the now poster child for entrepreneurial success in Chicago faced plenty of hardship gaining financial traction. "I started my firm here, and I was rejected by dozens and dozens of venture capital firms. I tracked it once and it was about ninety."

Thankfully for Jai, he recognized that he was going head-to-head with one of the core mechanisms of the Chicago innovation ecosystem, and that the calculated risk-taking tendencies of the venture firms didn't mean that the capital was lacking. He mentions, "One thing that's not true is the absence of funding. The money is there, but people aren't going to hand you bags of cash like they might do in the backseat of their car in the Valley." In Chicago, firms recognize that providing financial capital implies more than just money, it means putting forth all the resources available to assure that an organization has all the tools it needs to become successful.

These firms go the extra mile because they know they will be rewarded if they pay their due diligence. Chicago has the country's highest level of venture exits of over ten times the original investment, and that is a testament to both the work that these firms put into their startups, as well as their level of calculated risk in deciding to which organizations they should dedicate funds. This staggering level of return on investment isn't lost on other members of the Chicago innovation ecosystem. In fact, many types of organizations are changing the way they leverage their financial capital via a more collaborative, venture-focused mindset.

Venture-Focused Mindsets in Corporations

Though often one of the first stops for many budding startups, venture and private capital firms are not the only sources of financial capital in an innovation ecosystem. Large corporations have in recent years become a source of investment for young companies, having cultivated plenty of capital serving national, if not global, markets. Though large in stature, these companies know they are still vulnerable to competition, both from other like-sized corporations looking to steal market share, as well as startups bringing new technology that could render them obsolete.

More than ever before, corporations are creating their own venture divisions in order to stay relevant and agile in a fast-moving marketplace. Interestingly, many private capital firms don't see this as competition; if a large corporation wants to invest funds and resources to help one of the companies in a venture firm's portfolio, everyone's a winner (especially the startup). Kevin Willer, Co-founder and Partner at Chicago Ventures, brings this idea home: "If we could get our corporations to start buying into our local tech companies, that would boost the ecosystem. It would be great if local corporations bought local companies and had real exits."

It makes basic sense from an investment standpoint; put money into emerging prospects to help them get off the ground, and gain a return as they grow. The relationship is beneficial for both parties, and this mutual success is a magnet to other players in the ecosystem looking to facilitate the progress being made. Ed Wehmer saw the value that was being created in Chicago, and saw a role that his bank, Wintrust, could play by investing in investors. "We figured we should get involved with so much going on in innovation. A lot of the people who were backing these startups in innovation had a lot of money, and so we wanted to get to know them and have Chicago's bank be part of it."

Wintrust is just one of many large corporations across Chicago that have developed venture-minded divisions. They spend their days actively scouring the entrepreneurial landscape for high-opportunity startups to engage with. Whether it be through partnership, joint venture, merger, or acquisition, corporations are seeing that the best ideas don't always come from within their ivory towers; sometimes the best way to beat them is to join them.

An initiative like Chicago Innovation's Corporate Startup Matchmaking program can only exist within an ecosystem that thrives off of collaboration. It facilitates connections between large and small organizations with the mission to foster meaningful, mutually beneficial connections to inspire collaborative partnerships and drive regional growth.

The flow of financial capital doesn't just go from one source to one repository. Many players can bet on a single startup and bring a win for the entire table. When a community understands that local investments and exits benefit the entire city, the different entities work together for mutual prosperity instead of viewing each other as competition. Often times, however, the problem lies in the community's willingness to accept risk on a new venture.

Holly Copeland recognized that there was a role to play in being a first mover on the investment side of the coin when she was the Deputy Director for the Illinois State Office of Entrepreneurship, Innovation, and Technology. She was often willing to place bets on higher risk innovations and "leverage the resources of the state to make that investment." She explains, "Sometimes when you're dealing with innovation early on, people can be reluctant to put their money forward. So, in those cases, you can leverage government resources to have that pool of funding to deleverage the risk that might go with an idea, and then others are more inclined to contribute and jump into that effort."

When the multiple pillars of an ecosystem all lend a hand in promoting initiatives and partnerships, everyone wins. A combination of efforts from large corporations, small startups, government, venture capital firms, universities or nonprofits, a collaboratively focused ecosystem understands that the whole is greater than the sum of its parts. It's a simple mindset shift that changes the way different types of organizations work together.

On Equal Footing

The gentle oxpecker and robust rhinoceros might not compare in physical stature, but they share an equivalent role in their mutualistic relationship. Without one, the other would fall gravely ill in desperate search of a new partner or solution to fill the void. In the same way, though startups, large corporations, venture firms, universities, nonprofits, and others behave differently, they all play an equal role in sustaining the innovation ecosystem.

As Caralynn Nowinski Collens, CEO of Dimension Inx, identifies, there is a reinforcing cycle between leveraging capital to build talent. "I think that we constantly talk about the barrier with capital. I'm less of a cynic in that sense. Yes, we need more capital here, but we also need good deals here. But to get the good deals here, we need to get and keep the good people. I do think that we need to put some strategies in place for how we're going to recruit and retain the best talent." Bringing in top talent takes capital, and that talent can lead to future growth and success. One breeds the other, but neither is feasible without its partner. Everything is connected.

With a common goal of mutual prosperity, the different constituencies within the Chicago innovation ecosystem have developed a palpable infrastructure for the cultivation, development, transfer, and activation of human and financial capital. Whether it is to source seed funding to drive forward a juggernaut startup, or attract talented engineers from local universities into large corporations to modernize customer solutions, the pathways of capital flow are diverse and multifaceted.

The capital balance keeps everyone on a similar playing field and in good understanding of what one another has in terms of needs and excess. When this happens, organizations begin to develop relationships that extend past deal flows and handshakes; it fosters a community that shares a culture for collaboration. Communities that value collaboration take pride in seeing success come from these kinds of inter-organizational partnerships, and reverberate successes across the city as a sign that what they are trying to accomplish is working.

When regions are able to align under a shared value like collaboration and actively work to recognize the successes that come from partnerships, people and organizations begin to feel the need to become a part of what has developed around them. They want to not only contribute and benefit, but also be seen as contributors and beneficiaries. Through these dedicated efforts by individuals

Caralynn Nowinski Collens

CEO, Dimension Inx

Former CEO, MxD (formerly UI LABS)

Fun Fact:

As a graduate student, Caralynn co-founded SanoGene Therapeutics, an early-stage biotechnology company. As CEO, she led the company's spinout from the University of Illinois and raised a strategic equity investment.

and organizations to actively benefit the ecosystem as a whole, a new form of capital is cultivated; a social capital that exists purely as a means of "paying it forward."

CHAPTER
8
CHICAGO'S CULTURE CURRENCY

CHAPTER 8: CHICAGO'S CULTURE CURRENCY

On a late, rainy evening on the second of November 2016, something impossible happened in Chicago. For many of the forty million people worldwide who tuned into the seventh game of the World Series, the seventeen-minute rain delay at the end of the tied ninth inning felt longer than the 108 years it had taken for the Chicago Cubs to make it that close to a national title. As though a mythical prophecy had finally been fulfilled, the team's eventual victory bore truth to an unimaginable phenomenon often equated to hell freezing over or pigs flying. So much so, in fact, that over five million people made pilgrimage to Chicago's Grant Park for the Cubs' victory parade, forming the seventh-largest gathering of people in human history.

What brought that many people together was more than just winning a baseball game. The cultural significance of that moment was not only felt by every single person living in Chicago, but people around the world that understood what that championship meant to the city. Even rival White Sox fans couldn't deny the smallest feelings of celebration, though many were likely just happy to stop hearing their North-side-neighbors' mantra "there's always next year." For a brief moment, the city came together as one to celebrate the accomplishment of a collective goal over a century in the making. The significance of that championship and its ability to bring so many people together are just one example of the extremely powerful and profound culture present throughout Chicago, and sheds light on an important aspect of why the collective innovation ecosystem is thriving.

Creating and Sustaining a Culture of Innovation

"It starts with a culture," explains Sam Yagan, CEO of ShopRunner, in describing what makes up the innovation ecosystem. As one of the pioneers of the Internet dating industry and Founder of OkCupid, Sam knows a thing or two about bringing people together. He continues, "And then on top of the culture is the active participation and engagement in the different parts of the community." It is an underlying culture that creates the values-based foundation, on top of which are formed the guidelines for the actions and behaviors within the ecosystem.

The key words here from Sam are "active participation and engagement," terms often heard at the company level as key initiatives for motivating employees to become more passionate about their work. But while developing a fluid and innovative culture within an organization is hard enough for many corporations, Sam is talking about a citywide, 2.7 million-person culture that stretches across different neighborhoods and communities.

How is this possible? How could so many different people, organizations, and communities form a single culture and ecosystem, especially when their makeup is incredibly diverse? Howard Tullman suggests, "I don't know if there is any other city doing more than Chicago in terms of trying to create this new culture." In short, it takes a lot of work. But prior to exploring how Chicago's citywide culture of innovation has become so deeply infused into the many neighborhoods, industries, and sectors, it is important to come together under a single definition of the term "innovation culture."

Defining a "Culture of Innovation"

Upon hearing that a company has an innovative culture, one might conjure up images of open desk concepts, free food, foosball tables, beer taps, and the like. People are dressed casually, and most of their clothing has their company logo stitched somewhere on the front lapel. While these amenities might look good in a recruiting brochure, they often lack the depth and substance necessary to create a palpable community and culture.

Developing an organizational culture centered around innovation is no easy task. When done correctly, it can motivate and drive an entire workforce to rally together under a single cry. It gives everyone a common vision, goal, and understanding of not only what the company is trying to accomplish, but why. A culture of innovation is the collective set of values and norms that are shared among a group of people working towards a common goal of creating new value through solving problems.

Values represent a set of beliefs that describe what is most important to people. As Tom and Susan Kuczmarski describe in their book, *Lifting People Up: The Power of Recognition*, "Values influence the choices and decisions we make, the way we invest our energy and time, the people we choose to be close to, and the interests we pursue." Norms, on the other hand, are the physical manifestation behind these values. Continue the Kuczmarskis, "Norms serve as the 'translators' of values into daily behaviors and communications. Norms are group-decided codes of conduct. Without them, values can end up being just a list of beliefs." These two fundamental elements make up every single culture, from the workplace to school, and from church to home.

Applied correctly at an organization, an innovation culture can inspire rapid growth, empower employees, and bring a company into the fray as a market leader, all in the pursuit of a single vision and mission. As John Berschied, former head of R&D at Alberto Culver, is quoted in *Lifting People Up*, "When the culture is innovative, you are tapping into the total knowledge of the entire organization as opposed to selected bits and pieces." Once everyone understands not only their common goal, but the role that he or she plays in achieving it, they move collectively as a well-oiled machine. Consider, then, the potential when a collective of organizations, associations, government entities, and more come together to pursue a common goal for an entire region.

Values and Norms

In the lobby of most large corporations, just behind the reception desk, sits a plaque on the wall with five to ten words intended to encapsulate the values of the organization. Frequent chart-toppers are "integrity," "respect," and "commitment to excellence," with recent trends featuring "inclusion" and "boldness." And although these pleasant-sounding words might seem attractive to potential clients, shareholders, and recruiting firms, they are not always representative of the true beliefs that guide the culture of an organization.

Go down the hall beyond that reception desk and ask the next person what they think is important in the workplace. How do they think people should act and communicate? What real benefit do their work and company provide? Do they believe their peers and management feel the same way? Shockingly, the response might not accurately reflect the words on the wall, but they do speak to the real-world values that guide the culture of the office.

It's not always easy to articulate values because of their very nature as intangibles. Returning to *Lifting People Up*, "Culture can be extremely hard to change. Not only is it difficult to define something so intangible, but it can be challenging to identify the appropriate steps to turn a desired culture into a reality." Companies that struggle to transform their culture always seem to fall prey to this; they quickly learn that writing a series of idealistic words on the wall does not inspire change. The way to get a group of people to work together is by understanding the values that bind them, and then leveraging those common passions and beliefs to build a culture of which everyone wants to be a part.

There is no etched plaque or statue in the city of Chicago with the engraved words, "**C**ity pride, **H**umility, **I**nclusion, **C**alculated risk-taking, **A**ltruism, **G**rit, and **O**penness." If a group of people were asked what the values of Chicagoans are, they might give a plethora of different words or phrases that make up the complex belief system that is shared. But once they start talking about what is important to them and their city, how people should behave and interact, and how individuals work together to achieve communal goals, it becomes clear. The C.H.I.C.A.G.O. Way is a summation of the common values that are shared amongst a myriad of types of people within the business and innovation community.

But as with all aspects of life, talk in the business world is cheap. Culture is not influenced by how people feel; change requires action. This is where norms come into play. In an office space, valuing transparency is important for creating a trusting environment. However, the culture doesn't reflect that value unless people are communicating often and speaking openly about their problems alongside their successes.

In Chicago, Andrea Zopp notes that this culture is seen immediately when first setting foot in the city. She shares, "We have this corporate community where as soon as you get here, your fellow CEOs take you aside and say you need to join this club, this board, etc. It's hard to come here as a CEO and just sit on your haunches. Collaboration is in our history and culture." On a citywide ecosystem level, the norms that reinforce the culture of innovation are seen through the cultivation, distribution, and collection of social capital. It is the proof in the pudding; the money where the mouth is. It is the demonstration that someone

Andrea Zopp

President & CEO, World
Business Chicago

Former Deputy
Mayor of Chicago and
Chief Neighborhood
Development Officer

Former President & CEO,
Chicago Urban League

Fun Fact:

When she was appointed
Deputy Mayor in 2016,
Andrea also became
the city's first-ever
Chief Neighborhood
Development Officer.

believes so much in a mission that he or she is willing to lend their time, advice, and (at times) funding to promote a community to achieve more.

Social Capital

The saying, "actions speak louder than words" is doubly true when talking about influencing a culture. People at every level from the CEO all the way down to the frontline workers understand the difference between talk and action. Not everyone has what it takes to deliver on their promises, and when it comes to giving time, money, and resources to social or societal programs, that tends to count for double. That is why when talking about the importance of developing a citywide community and ecosystem around innovation, having people and institutions produce, develop, and deliver on social capital is on par with (if not more vital than) financial and human capital.

This resource is vital for places like Chicago, where collaboration and interaction are a part of the ecosystem's DNA. In comparison to other cities, Chicago's progress hasn't rested solely on the shoulders of a few change-makers, it has been a large-scale effort from the entire community. Chris Gladwin, CEO of Ocient, explains, "It is a testament to the growth of the Chicago innovation ecosystem that there isn't a specific individual that has been the reason for the city's growth."

Broadly, social capital refers to the time, resources, and effort that people devote to furthering the mission of the community. It manifests itself in a variety of ways, and can have fluctuating levels of impact and reach. It is seen both on an individual level and through companies, and can be revenue-generating or philanthropic. Social capital also often works in tandem with the other two forms of capital, human and financial. Some examples include:

- Coalitions, associations, and clubs forming with the expressed intention of advancing the ecosystem (e.g. P33, Chicago Innovation, the Economic Club of Chicago, Vistage)
- Large organizations making in-kind or financial donations to nonprofits and civic groups
- A CEO lending his or her scarce free time to mentor an employee
- An entrepreneur being recognized by a civic awards program (e.g. Momentum Awards, Moxie Awards, Chicago Innovation Awards)
- A large corporation drafting a strategic alliance with a startup
- A nonprofit organization working in conjunction with local businesses to raise awareness for a cause
- An incubator partnering with a university to give students the resources to grow their ideas into real businesses

The phrase "cultivating social capital" might not be on the minds of the various people and organizations taking these sorts of actions, but "building a culture" certainly is. Going the extra mile to help or work with another person is what transforms a city into an ecosystem. It's the collaborative nature of people that makes big sweeping changes possible, and these large-scale changes are only possible through a commonly understood goal. Each of these interactions, connections, and partnerships combine to form a network of people with a culture that drives them forward.

The Power of the Network

The job description for the Chief Information Officer for an entire state seems largely impossible for one person to accomplish. How does a single individual manage to assess, progress, and invest in an entire conglomerate of different organizations throughout a region with a common vision or goal for them to collectively achieve?

As Hardik Bhatt, former CIO for the State of Illinois, explains, "In Chicago and in general, you have to make the investment to build relationships. You have to invest a lot of time and energy,

Hardik Bhatt

Leader, Digital
Government, Amazon
Web Services

Former CIO, State of
Illinois

Uber

*"My parents moved to
Chicago in their sixties,
and my dad doesn't
drive downtown. At
seventy-three years old,
he continues to work and
doesn't have to depend on
me to drive him. It's a very
liberating innovation."*

One of Chicago's most
valuable cross-sector
assets, Hardik has led
innovation at the city and
state levels, and has also
held tech leadership roles
at Amazon, Cisco, and
Oracle.

and then you can build relationship capital." Like any form of capital, social capital does not grow on trees; building it requires making investments into relationships with others. Over time, these relationships will pay dividends in the form of shared goals and priorities, as well as a willingness to help others succeed. This can manifest as a helpful connection or introduction, public recognition of an impressive feat or milestone, or a simple favor. It's a simple concept: get to know people on a personal level, and then help one another achieve future goals.

For Hardik, building social or as he calls it, "relationship capital," is an investment into a community. He defines his investment in terms of "what have I put into all of these relationships? It's the time, energy, everything that you do to make others successful." And a lot of time needs to be invested to form these relationships.

For those to whom extroversion comes naturally, going out and meeting people in the community is often a daily or weekly ritual. But building social capital speaks to something greater than cocktails and small-talk networking. It involves devoting time to get to know people on a deeper level and sharing personal issues and company challenges. Allowing for vulnerability and building this closeness works because people can't work to help one another without understanding their gripes and issues.

Hardik realized this necessity as soon as he took the office in 2006. "Prior to being the CIO, all I did was work and go home. Since becoming the CIO, I am much more well networked in Chicago. The credit goes to the Mayor's Council of Technology Advisors. We had so many good people in those meetings and so much key information was shared.

After those meetings, I got more interested in what was happening with groups like Chicago Innovation, the Economic Club, and the Executives' Club."

The more organizations and groups Hardik joined, the more he found himself immersed in what was evolving into the Chicago innovation ecosystem. "It automatically builds that capital up, and in time you reap the rewards of those relationships. I have seen a lot of people utilizing it for organizational success or even on the state level." People sharing stories, lending advice and funding, and getting to know everything that was going on in Chicago was an unintentional instigator in growing the ecosystem to what it is today.

Building networks leads to more than just introductions, as well. These relationships yield new ventures, businesses, associations, and more. As Fieldglass Founder Jai Shekhawat describes, when you build a trusting business relationship with someone, it lasts until the very end. "I'll promise you that if we make it, we'll all cross the finish line together. Which means we'll sell our shares at the same time. We'll make our money at the same time, and it won't be me cutting some side deal with someone, which happens all too often." Once people started realizing that these social capital investments actually paid dividends, it started becoming a much more intentional endeavor.

A Town Full of Teams

When the Chicago Innovation Awards was founded in 2002, its initial goal was simply to shine a spotlight on some of the successful innovators and entrepreneurs that Chicago had to offer. The intent was to give Midwestern entrepreneurs a rare opportunity for recognition that too often gravitated towards the coast, and provide a haven to be proud of what they had accomplished. As Michael Krauss, Co-founder of Market Strategy Group, puts it, "What Tom Kuczmarski and Dan Miller did with Chicago Innovation, by really catalyzing the community and focusing it around an awards program, was crucial."

The crucial element in this celebratory endeavor was the formation of a community, albeit small at first, that shared a common viewpoint that innovation was for everyone and deserved to be celebrated. Within this community, the Chicago Innovation Awards (CIA) was able to shine a spotlight on people and companies that exemplified the Chicago innovation ecosystem at its best. The platform for recognition that the awards program built was, at the end of the day, a social capital-cultivating endeavor. With the goal of promoting the ecosystem and elevating members of the society that exemplified the city's innovative, hardworking values, the CIA deposited social capital into each winner that stepped on stage at the Goodman and Harris Theaters. This capital paid dividends over time for its recipients; now in its nineteenth year, 98 percent of CIA winners are still in business, and forty-six have been acquired for exit values exceeding $90 billion. The platform has also helped winners raise billions of dollars in capital after winning their awards.

Fast-forward to today, Chicago Innovation has expanded to more than just awards. The organization now hosts a yearlong series of events and programs geared towards educating, connecting, and celebrating innovators in the Chicago region. Embracing the idea that recognition isn't the only form of social capital that can be fostered, Chicago Innovation has grown into a community of innovators and entrepreneurs that help one another promote ideas and values. As Hardik Bhatt describes, "What Chicago Innovation is doing is critical. They are creating the opportunity to network for the people. It's up to the individual; you can be a passive part of it, or you can be an active participant and get the most out of it as possible." The creation of an active and engaged community centered around innovation is what allows social capital to flourish and become fully integrated into how people interact.

People like Mike Rothman, Founder and Chairman of SMS Assist, are able to learn so much about the communities around them thanks to these types of awards programs. He shares, "SMS Assist was fortunate enough to win a 2012 Chicago Innovation Award, which opened my eyes to see the vast number of companies who competed for it." Because of these grand-scale recognition programs, people are able to learn about other innovators, and better collaborate with those chasing similar goals.

This includes meeting new partners, vendors, clients, acquisition candidates, service providers, and more. Chicago Innovation is far from the only group in the city that works to develop a community of like-minded thinkers helping one another succeed and innovate. In fact, on any given evening there are tens of different organizations hosting events with the hopes that their cultivation of social capital will pay dividends later on.

For some groups like Chicago Ideas and Chicago Inno, events are the means through which they sow seeds of social capital. Casting as wide a net as possible, Chicago Ideas strives to bring people together to think big and make moves towards solving major issues. Whether it be an event or discussion on the future of the healthcare industry, peace in the Middle East, or experiencing nirvana through chi alignment, their ultimate goal is to enact major change through a community rallying around ideas and initiatives. Chicago Inno's focus generally lies within the tech-startup vertical within the city. With events and communication focusing on the next waves of technology and industry trends, along with public recognition of venture funding, their hope is to follow the promotion and rise of a company from garage to unicorn. By publicly recognizing these future disruptors, much like the Chicago Innovation Awards, they provide a roadmap and role models for like-minded entrepreneurs to achieve success.

When a region is faced with big problems, it takes big initiatives to solve them. Planning the future of Chicago's tech infrastructure is a big problem, and the team trying to assemble the efforts to solve it is P33. They have gathered together executives and leaders from the private sector to figure out where Chicago needs to go next from a technological and economic development perspective. Their goal of making Chicago the most dynamic technology ecosystem by 2033 will require pooling the collective efforts of the hundreds of engaged professionals. This type of people-fueled movement is making constant deposits into the social capital piggy bank for the ecosystem to withdraw from in the next decade.

On the public side of the coin, World Business Chicago is getting the word out to the rest of the world about the progress the city has been making. With no shortage of bad PR on a national scale, Chicago needs champions like this to share inspiring stories and change the narrative of the region. While these different groups and teams are all working to achieve their own distinct missions, visions, goals, and communities, a success for one of them means success for all.

Inclusion Trumps Competition

Chicago is truly a town of teams, but unlike the Cubs and White Sox, these teams are not rivals. The key ingredient to an ecosystem is cohesion, and the many groups working to grow the innovation community understand that the sum of the parts is greater than the whole. That is why instead of endorsing exclusivity, these teams partner with one another readily to create a more integrated community. The overlap between members of the Economic Club, Executives' Club, P33, 1871, and Chicago Innovation communities alone is staggering. As the innovation ecosystem continues to flourish and grow, the members of these various subcommunities develop and become further integrated. The Venn diagram overlapping the people within the different groups becomes closer and closer to a circle.

Innovation is for everyone, whether they be a large corporation, a startup or a nonprofit. These people and more need to be a part of the conversation, and that means more than just a seat at the table. In order to bring everyone into the culture conversation, there needs to be a consistent effort towards welcoming in people and groups sitting beyond the fringe of the ecosystem edge.

It takes more than networking and recognizing the success of others. While these are crucial to further ingraining an existing culture, once the goal becomes to elevate the city to become a global leader, it takes some elbow grease. As Michael Krauss of Market Strategy Group puts it, "It can't be just local clubbiness. We have to create first-rate startups and connect them with our established companies, but they have to be best of breed."

There is a major talent pool that is ready to make an impact and be a part of the larger community, but it struggles to do so as a result of a number of different factors. Whether it be a close-knit ecosystem that is difficult to penetrate from the outside, or barriers to getting enough funding to properly scale an organization, groups often have trouble fulfilling their dreams because of roadblocks stopping them before they leave the starting gate. That's why it's so crucial to look at those who are creating an impact on the local level, and making significant improvements for a select number of people. Ecosystems don't grow and expand through just grand-scale change and big conversations; a major part of fostering social capital and deepening the culture is making a grassroots, localized impact.

Localized Impact

There is a quote by Vincent Van Gogh that reads, "Great things are not done by impulse, but by a series of small things brought together." A churning ecosystem of innovation produces and leverages a constant stream of social, financial, and human capital coming and going from multiple sources. It is spoken about often as a singular entity, but in truth there is no single ecosystem; it is an immense conglomerate of individuals and organizations doing their part to make the region better on a case-by-case basis.

Of all organizations making socially conscious, localized impact, the nonprofit sector stands apart from the rest. Aside from the amazing work done by groups fighting inequality, homelessness, poverty, disease, and so forth to make the world a better place, there are extremely significant nonprofits and foundations focused specifically on the development and prosperity of the Chicago innovation ecosystem.

For some fortunate individuals, the cards are already set at the table. They have at their disposal the network, the talent, the timing, and the funding to get a business off the ground, and are able to focus their time and hard work on bringing the company to the next level. Their time is spent optimizing products, interacting with customers, communicating with shareholders, and meeting their hiring goals. For others, starting a business is not as simple as lighting a match. Ranging from issues like a lack of connections or network, to difficulty gaining funding because of systemic inequality, many entrepreneurs spend more of their time searching for help and resources than they do on their sprouting businesses.

That's where groups like the Women's Business Development Center (WBDC) come in. Hedy Ratner founded the Chicago-based organization in 1986 with the mission to provide programs and services to support and accelerate women's business ownership, and strengthen the impact of women on the economy by creating jobs, fueling economic growth, and building strong communities. Now the largest, oldest, and most comprehensive women's business assistance center in the U.S., the group has truly "changed the face of business," as Hedy puts it.

In a time where inclusion is talked about in business more than ever, there is an enormous large-scale initiative to provide access, funding, and resources to underprivileged groups of people to help them get their great ideas and businesses off the ground and become a part of the ecosystem. While there still remains work to be done, the current climate is leaps and bounds ahead of where it once was. Hedy describes this shift in access: "There's been a massive increase in venture capital opportunities for women-owned businesses by women establishing capital funds. This is enormously helpful for growing innovative businesses for women who weren't even being considered at the time. They weren't necessarily gigantic developments like Amazon and Google, but they were interesting. They were innovative."

Financial capital is an inescapable hurdle that every entrepreneur must overcome, and sometimes it takes a substantial effort from a social impact perspective to make that funding more accessible. This overlap in the development and distribution of social and financial capital gets to the heart of how an innovation ecosystem can become more inclusive.

While the WBDC may have been a trailblazer in this effort, they are no longer alone. Today, Hedy describes how she works with "many organizations like the Federation of Women Contractors, the Illinois Hispanic Chamber of Commerce, World Business Chicago, and certainly Chicago Innovation, which has been a really successful partnership that continues to grow. We partner with groups so that we can help encourage more and more women to participate in this economic innovation ecosystem." These organizations that work together to drive social impact are not doing it just through helping people source financial capital either; there is a massive overlap in the development of social and human capital as well.

Bridging Human and Social Capital

When people work together to create a community in which everyone can thrive, it provides otherwise excluded people with the tools and resources to make a difference. Although it certainly does help, money isn't always the answer when it comes to improving a community. If people can't take proper advantage of the investments made, the finances are essentially worthless. One type of solution for providing dedicated alternative resources to those in need are workforce development groups like Cara and i.c.stars that create training programs for underprivileged communities. They are directly responsible for helping people advance their careers and livelihoods in ways that would otherwise be impossible.

Sandee Kastrul's organization, i.c.stars provides training programs so people from impoverished communities can learn technical skills. She sees firsthand the societal barriers that hinder these kinds of people as well as ex-convicts trying to create a better life for themselves. "The laws around ex-offenders are archaic. Laws like these and others around property taxes or school funding are great examples of things that hurt our communities. These are things that have to change. If I can't live in a decent place, have food, clothing and shelter, and feel safe, I may as well be planning on going back to prison. These laws push people back into the prison system." Sandee sees a greater good that can be done for these people that are searching for a better life, as well as the greater good that these people can do for others.

Led by President and CEO Maria Kim, Cara helps people affected by poverty obtain and keep high quality jobs, and to date has helped over ten thousand people secure a job. Their values speak to a higher level of work, as they strive to "rebuild hope, self-esteem, and opportunity" for individuals, and importantly "produce a profound social return on investment, where for every dollar invested in their work, $5.97 is reinvested into society over a five-year time horizon." This is social capital incarnate; creating an impact on a localized, even person-to-person basis that in time yields over fivefold benefits to the community.

At the end of the day, the work that Cara and i.c.stars do is not charity, it is workforce development. The people that are going through these programs might not come from wealth or may have faced setbacks or made mistakes in the past, but they have the capacity to develop into talented employees for companies at a time when the need for human capital is so critical. They become salespeople, programmers, customer relations professionals, and even start their own businesses. And in so doing, become enveloped in the ecosystem thanks to the work of these nonprofits.

The Capital Drives the Culture

Social capital is intangible and can be difficult to measure. It might seem like a nice-to-have effort in an ecosystem, but not nearly as important as the "real stuff." And this might be true on an individual level; a single person might be able to navigate the difficult pathways of bootstrapping a startup without anyone's help. Another person might be able to rise up the ranks of a corporation, eventually become the CEO, and bring that organization into a new era of success on his or her own. But in terms of looking out the window and creating a community or an ecosystem centered around innovation, it just can't happen without a culture.

A culture is what brings a community together to strive for a universal goal, and what helps people with similar problems band together to solve them as one. John Flavin puts it in perfect terms when he says, "What has been attractive about Chicago is that it has a mission-based mindset for people. These are not mercenaries you are bringing in. They are mission driven. They are joining something because they want to make an impact. There is something to be said for the Midwestern culture in that regard; it is the brain and the heart together. That's why I stay here in Chicago."

That culture is why the city's clout as a center for innovation has grown so much in such a relatively short amount of time. The city and the ecosystem aren't finished yet, however, and there is still much to accomplish. This will take more than incremental improvements. To maintain this rapid growth rate, Chicago's innovation ecosystem will need to break new ground.

CHAPTER
9
SUSTAINING
THE ECOSYSTEM

CHAPTER 9: SUSTAINING THE ECOSYSTEM

Over the last couple decades, the Chicago innovation ecosystem has grown at an accelerated rate. Today, the city is at a pivotal point of self-reflection and continued growth, poised for success as a global innovation hub. Ross Manire, former President and CEO of ExteNet Systems, reinforces, "We've got what it takes to make this work. The question is, are we going to be smart enough to take Chicago to the next level?" Growth only lasts so long, and each wave crashes down eventually. In the pursuit of seamlessly transitioning from the current wave to the next, there must be a clear strategy for sustaining the level of growth that has been captured. In short, the city needs to focus on more than just what is working today in order to grow tomorrow.

The need for forward thinking is seen across all forms of business; if a company focuses only on maintaining their current offerings, the revenues on existing products will decrease over time. More of the same will not inspire growth. Much like a company, a regional ecosystem must find a balance between maintaining successful ventures and breaking new ground.

By its very nature, an innovation ecosystem has no overhead manager. A collective of players, ranging in sector, industry, and size, this coalition must work as a whole to advance its cause. Just as a team is made up of individuals playing various roles, each pillar of the ecosystem needs to have a different goal in order to increase its contribution to the remaining members. Together, these goals form a blueprint for how to sustain the growth of the ecosystem.

The Blueprint for Sustained Ecosystem Growth:

1. Corporations Nurture
2. Government Convenes
3. Talent Creators Develop
4. Nonprofits Collaborate
5. Funders Reinvest
6. Entrepreneurs Give Back
7. Everyone Tells Chicago's Story

1. Corporations Nurture

"A lot of large companies are recognizing that they can help foster growth by making investments into organizations that are tangential to their organization. Their investments and acquisitions are vital."

Ross Manire, Former President & CEO of ExteNet Systems

Ross Manire

Former President & CEO, ExteNet Systems

Fun Fact:

Before founding eventual Chicago Innovation Award winner ExteNet Systems, Ross led the sale of two tech companies for a total exit value of just under $1.2 billion.

Despite Chicago's roots as a corporate town, there is still a need for the largest companies to become more involved in the community that surrounds them. With the highest rate of corporate relocations in the country, Chicago is welcoming more and more Fortune 500 organizations to the region each year. To date, Chicago is home to more than four hundred major corporate headquarters, including thirty-six in the Fortune 500. These companies have a responsibility to the city in which they call home, just as the ecosystem they enter has a responsibility to reach out and bring them into the fold.

Chicago's strength in business-to-business (B2B) enterprises and its diversity in sector go hand in hand; as companies develop solutions to help one another solve problems, the community as a whole prospers. An interesting dynamic is how the size of a company can play a role in these interactions. Says Brenna Berman, "We get so much done in Chicago because the tech ecosystem is made up of large companies, small startups, and mid-sized businesses." Just as the diversity of industry is an asset to the region, as is the sundry breakdown of startups, corporations, and everything in between. The balance of human and financial capital between large and small organizations takes this to the next level when considering the

David Weinstein

Founder & CEO,
Freshwater Advisors

Former Founding
President, Chicagoland
Entrepreneurial Center

Favorite Innovation:

Cleversafe

Cleversafe is a leading
provider of Cloud Object
Storage, acquired by IBM
in 2015 for $1.3 billion.

*"Cleversafe actually splits
up data into eleven
different pieces so that
if seven go down, you
can still reconstruct
the data and move
from unsustainable to
sustainable technology."*

Fun Fact:

David spearheaded the
creation of Mayor Daley's
Council of Technology
Advisors, cited by many
interviewees for this
book as a major catalyst
for the city's innovation
ecosystem.

total net impact that can come from the two types of businesses working together.

David Weinstein is someone who has felt the direct impact of large corporations working with small organizations. "Larry Levy was my first million-dollar client," he shares. "He was choosing between a well-known company and me, a startup. He said to his team, 'If nobody gave me a chance, you guys wouldn't be sitting here.'" Every successful company starts with a first sale. Because of that single contract, David was able to grow his tech startup BlueMeteor into a viable business. For young organizations in search of early customers, a contract with a corporation can literally make or break the company. As the ecosystem continues to churn out startups left and right, it's crucial that corporations recognize the power they have to help these businesses get off the ground.

Exelon, one of the nation's largest energy providers, is a prime example of a corporate steward in the Chicago innovation ecosystem. For this organization, innovation and investment go hand in hand as a strategy for growth. Exelon's "Dancing with Startups," is an initiative that helps put local startups on display for the $36 billion energy company, so that they can become introduced to leaders of various business units. Nearly six years after the program's launch, Exelon has continued collaborating with many of these startups after their initial introduction.

Another way that corporations like Exelon can connect with Chicago's innovative startups is through their support for incubators. Sandee Kastrul notes, "Now enterprise companies are leasing space in the incubators because everyone wants to be a part of it." Exelon and Chicago Ventures both have office spaces mere feet away from one another in 1871. Talk about creating an environment where startups can thrive! Large corporations have the potential to rub shoulders with the very startups that could be developing solutions to their complex problems.

On the flip side, groups like Technori, Techstars, and the Chicago Innovation Corporate Startup Matchmaking program act as showcases for these startups so their voices can be heard by corporate behemoths. For years, it has been a struggle for these talented but feeble entrepreneurs to wade through bureaucracy and hierarchy to finally get in front of the right buyer at a large company to pitch their solutions. But if a region is committed to empowering startups, corporations need to support initiatives such as these to reduce the effort it takes for entrepreneurs to make a case for why they should exist.

Corporations also have the ability to leverage their networks to rally people together under a single cause. For example, Exelon recently launched a $20 million climate change investment initiative, targeting startups developing technologies that address the global threat. This sends a message to the community that environmental issues are crucial and need to be dealt with, and it actually does something to solve the problem.

As corporations look to advance the culture and business ecosystem, they need to spearhead similar initiatives focused on innovation and entrepreneurship. Their capacity for impact is far more powerful than many of the other levels of the ecosystem because of their resources, reach, and size of audience. Long gone are the days when the largest companies could sit in their ivory campuses with corporate moats separating them from the rest of the ecosystem.

As the innovation ecosystem continues to flourish, corporations need to play a bigger role in connecting with various startups, universities, and nonprofits, as well as rally others in the corporate community to do the same. But, like innovation at the corporate level, things only get done when people at the senior level buy into the idea. Though Chicago is home to many community leaders who are engaged to support the growth of the ecosystem, they will need to play larger roles in the future if the ecosystem is to continue on its current path.

2. Government Convenes

It is critical that the government not only adamantly supports the initiatives focused on growing Chicago's innovation ecosystem, but also becomes more actively involved with the organizations that drive its growth. This requires a keen understanding of the strengths and weaknesses of the region, and formulating clearly communicated plans on how to achieve goals. The diversity of today's economy is a clear asset in many respects, as it presents opportunities for businesses to collaborate to create enterprise solutions without overtly competing with one another. It is a formula for collaborative growth. However, some in the city hold the opinion that an even-keeled economy mitigates single industries from advancing to the point of global leadership.

It is a valid concern of many that Chicago might become a jack of all trades, but master of none if significant focus isn't put toward particular industrial areas in which the city believes it can be a global leader. In this respect, both P33 and Mayor Lori Lightfoot have created different plans to focus on four areas where the government can lend additional support. With a mix of public and private sector leaders on various committees, P33 aims to ensure that the city is a leader in a few industries that are critical to its success. They are focusing their efforts on four areas where Chicago is poised to win: food and agriculture, industry 4.0, health and life sciences, and data and platform businesses. They believe that with a focus on these four key industries, as well as a desire to build strategies to scale innovation, they can take Chicago to the next level.

On the other hand, Mayor Lori Lightfoot's plan focuses in on the industrial and manufacturing sector, food processing, and professional and corporate services. "We need to maintain our leadership position in these industries and connect our residents to available jobs," Mayor Lightfoot proclaimed at a press conference. Still in her first year in office, the impacts of Mayor Lightfoot's plan have yet to be seen, but she is blazing a new trail in terms of leveraging the power of the government to make an impact on local businesses that have for so long been underappreciated.

As Hedy Ratner shares, the government and its agencies have the tools to make major impact for private businesses: "The Small Business Administration can be enormously helpful in providing support and technical assistance." Hedy's extensive work lobbying for government programs to aid underserved populations has paid dividends to many in Chicago. Whether working with local governments to craft the Community Reinvestment Act or with nationally focused causes, Hedy has inspired many in the government to make a difference. "That's where the leadership at the federal and local levels in government can help. The National Women's Council helped to start encouraging businesses to grow through equity and venture capital investment." As more and more government initiatives grant aid and resources to small businesses, a proliferation of successful new ventures will be apparent.

The major entity in Chicago connecting the city with local and global enterprises is World Business Chicago (WBC). Currently led by Andrea Zopp, WBC acts as a megaphone for Chicago on a global scale, attracting businesses from overseas and fostering direct connections with local enterprises. They work closely with the mayor, Chicago Sister Cities International, and the ChicagoNEXT council of technology leaders. The potential for impact on businesses is enormous, as Kevin Willer recalls, thinking back to his early days with Google: "I remember Dan Lyne from WBC stopped by. He said he handled tech for the government and asked if we needed help. He helped get us credibility and put a spotlight on us." It didn't take long for this spotlight to get global attention, and the municipal organization hopes to foster several Googles in the near future.

World Business Chicago's mission to keep the city in the global conversation is a crucial one, and Hardik Bhatt explains how bringing businesses to the area is going to be key if the city plans on breaking new ground. He notes, "If we want to be successful in areas like autonomous cars, we need our government to create a more business-friendly environment to attract companies that are building in core tech." The government, he says, can create an environment that will support local businesses through the difficult challenge of navigating brand-new industries by working to bring in more companies and talent.

The government's impact as it relates to supporting the ecosystem's talent creators needs to continue to be addressed as well. Illinois is home to some great public universities, and, as Caralynn Nowinski Collens notes, government investment into universities is key. "The amount of government dollars that are poured into universities to create new innovations is tremendous. These universities have a big role to feed the city's innovations both through student entrepreneurs and effective talent." Investment dollars can only do so much, however. There is a need for the talent creators to step up in the next phase of the ecosystem as well.

3. Talent Creators Develop

"The key thing to focus on next is how do you build the next generation of leaders? We need those people at the table now."

**Hardik Bhatt, Leader of Digital Government,
Amazon Web Services**

In innovation, it's a constant race to be first to market. The phrase, "If you're on time, you're late, and if you're late, you're forgotten" holds completely true. That means that the next generation of innovators needs to get started sooner and faster if they want to compete in today's ecosystem. The city needs to invest in programs to inspire innovation and entrepreneurship, as well as instill the values of "The C.H.I.C.A.G.O. Way" into the city's youth.

Starting when they are young, students in Chicago are given many opportunities to succeed. Today, Chicago Public School (CPS) students are achieving at record levels. According to CPS, 89.4 percent of freshman high school students were on track to graduate, and $1.33 billion in scholarships were earned in 2018. As these students continue to develop, the city is working to make college more accessible in a day and age when tuition costs are a major barrier. If a student maintains a B average, they get access to community college for free. If they can maintain those grades for long enough, they are granted access to several leading universities in the city for half price.

There is a massive amount of talent in underserved areas of Chicago. "The brightest minds are across the cities and in the neighborhoods," says Brian Bannon, former CEO of the Chicago Public Library. Facilitating the growth of young creative thinkers and problem solvers will continue to be important as Chicago continues to grow. Brian notes that, "The more we can look to the whole city as a source for talent that will drive our future success, and the more effectively we can get that talent connected to the right structures to shape and hone their skills, the more successful we will be."

Brian's successor, Commissioner of the Chicago Public Library Andrea Telli, is laying the groundwork to continue expanding educational programming across the city. To build the city's local talent to the level it needs to be to make Chicago a global leader, it takes more organizations like the Chicago Public Library that are focused on developing talent. In order to continue along this path of growth, the entire city will need to continue to engage the talent that is created here, supporting the hardest working students and most effective employees. As Terry Savage succinctly adds, "You can't continue forward unless you bring along kids and underachievers."

As these talented students become working professionals, there must be concerted efforts to encourage engineers and business-builders to stay in Chicago. As Sam Yagan states, "I don't think we have yet to establish ourselves as the go-to place for Midwestern tech talent." As it stands today, some young, motivated, hard-working employees are leaving Chicago to go find work elsewhere. To retain that talent, there is a great need to develop employees, keep them motivated, and offer them favorable living and working conditions to encourage them to stay in the city.

Too often in the talent conversation, the focus is put solely on recent graduates as the target for retention and hiring. As Harper Reed, former CTO of Threadless reminds us, there is a massive population of potential employees that are often overlooked. A group he coins as "Motorola Engineers." He describes them as "Mid-career people that have families, aren't going to be a startup engineer, and are very talented. You have ten thousand engineers just sitting right there. All you have to do is give them a good pitch that doesn't include working twenty-four hours a day, and they'd love to work with you." Top-tier engineers are scarce, and while there needs to be a focus on encouraging young people to stay in the Midwest, there is also a silver lining to young Chicagoans voyaging west after graduation.

Howard Tullman, former CEO of 1871 and former Executive Director of the Kaplan Institute, sees the benefit of working with people that have a little less green behind their ears. In response to concerns of tech talent leaving the city for the coasts, he reassures, "We're starting to see this boomerang effect of people coming back with three to eight years of experience." He even encourages young talent to experience the difference in Silicon Valley's culture, and thanks the organizations for training these Chicagoans "on their dime." Howard is confident that the Midwestern culture of innovation is too good to pass up for long. The truth is, in many aspects the living conditions in Chicago are especially favorable for people on a tight budget. Sam Yagan notes that "Chicago is a very livable city, relative to Los Angeles, San Francisco, and New York City." Andrea Zopp adds, "Especially as the coasts get more congested and expensive, we have some real elasticity in our economy."

Large corporations can also support the community through their investment in the city's talent. Sandee Kastrul says, "Big companies can invest in the community and find people who think differently. Diversity of thought, experience, and age help these employees solve problems." With such an ample supply of talent across the city, corporations have the opportunity to attract high-achieving, passionate, and engaged employees.

SMS Assist is a prime example of a Chicago-based company that focuses on attracting talent and developing them internally to create future leaders. Marc Shiffman was employee number twenty-five at SMS Assist back in 2010. Ten years later, he is the CEO. Marc constantly uses his story as a prime example of how a company can provide high-quality individuals at an organization with the resources and opportunities they need to grow.

Chicago needs to maintain its focus on talent in order to continue the success in developing the ecosystem. Starting with youth and moving onward through retirement, there are numerous opportunities for developing, attracting, retaining, and motivating people to contribute more to their schools, organizations, and communities. If organizations can even further turn their focus to helping people grow and making an impact, it will pay enormous dividends for the region in the future.

4. Nonprofits Collaborate

Chicago is home to some of the largest nonprofits and foundations in the country. In order to sustain the ecosystem, these types of organizations need to support one another in the same way that they support the community. By their very nature as providers of grants or services, nonprofits are accustomed to working with members of their community to help them reach goals or solve problems. However, there can be a sense of competition among nonprofits. In fairness, there is only so much money and sponsorship that a city's donors can provide. Each nonprofit is technically in competition for a share of that funding. But, if an organization is truly cause-based, it should be able to put this mentality aside for the benefit of the greater community. If these groups can change their perception and consider one another partners instead of competitors, it will allow for bigger initiatives and movements that will inevitably bring more fundraising capital to the region.

Benefit Chicago is a terrific example of what can be achieved through nonprofit collaboration. It was formed in 2017 when three organizations came together after recognizing the potential impact they could provide as a combined front. The MacArthur Foundation, the Chicago Community Trust, and the Calvert Impact Capital partnered to create Benefit Chicago: a $100 million fund aimed at bridging the gap between individuals who seek to invest in their community and organizations who are looking for patient, risk-tolerant capital. These three organizations brought their resources together to create something that could not have been done otherwise. Julia Stasch, former President of the MacArthur Foundation explains why she invested in the partnership effort: "We live in Chicago. We see the need here. There are organizations that do heroic work every day, in every community." These are the types of organizations that these three foundations have come together to support: groups that are working hard to impact their surroundings and build a positive future.

This is the spirit of Chicago that needs to stay in order for the ecosystem to become a global innovation powerhouse. Both for-profit and nonprofit enterprises need to think about building wealth, creating jobs, upskilling workers, and contributing to the community at large. This has become a responsibility and expectation of members of the business community.

Again, this isn't charity for the sake of good public relations or Facebook likes. This propensity for social impact is guided by a pragmatic Chicago culture. In the same vein that risk-taking in business or venture capital is heavily measured and calculated, the same is true for grand-scale philanthropic or social investments into the region. "Benefit Chicago unleashes a different type of philanthropic capital," says Terry Mazany, former President and

CEO of the Chicago Community Trust. He reinforces, "It is a capital that has some type of return." Led by Executive Director William Towns, Benefit Chicago brings organizations together to build social good, but does so in a sustainable way that yields downstream returns. It is this type of innovative collaboration across sector that builds up Chicago and supports underserved communities.

Another example of a potential model for nonprofit collaboration is Forefront, a statewide association that represents grant-makers and nonprofits. This community is eleven hundred members strong and brings together nonprofits and their funders through events and business development initiatives. They are moving the needle forward by encouraging socially-minded people across the city to collaborate. This is the type of organization that inspires community activism and growth among the business and nonprofit communities. Groups like theirs therefore need continued support, and need to continuously support one another.

In some cases, nonprofits are taking a note from the entrepreneurial activity in the for-profit sector. Former Chicago Bear Israel Idonije has been a philanthropic champion in the city ever since he retired from the National Football League. He is partnering with Forefront, The Field Foundation, Woods Fund, and United States Artists to develop a new philanthropic innovation center. FBRK Impact House is an incubator-like space that will unite grantors, entrepreneurs, and innovators. The center is designed to become the world's largest innovation-focused philanthropy center, dedicated to serving communities in need. CEO of City Tech Collaborative Brenna Berman notes that Chicago nonprofits are no stranger to innovative thinking: "We have philanthropies that care about and invest in tech innovation."

Not all nonprofits are charities; some of the most impactful organizations are ones that bring people together and make connections. The Discovery Partners Institute (DPI) is a new initiative hoping to do just that. The forward-thinking collaborative aims to "bring hundreds of the best minds from academia and industry together in an interdisciplinary hub of unprecedented critical mass" to accelerate innovation and create life-changing products, taking them to market faster than ever before. DPI focuses on four key areas: culture and society, entrepreneurship and technology transfer, education and workforce development, and public policy. This collaboration will facilitate greater interest in Chicago, inspire additional investment into collaborative partnerships, and maintain a problem-oriented innovation mindset across sectors.

These types of cross-industry, for-profit and nonprofit collaborations are key to the continued growth of the ecosystem. The Chicago Innovation Foundation is a nonprofit that exists to empower innovators and entrepreneurs in the ecosystem and ensure that innovation is for everyone. The foundation is largely supported by the corporate sector, whose sponsorships make possible the various programs focused on educating, connecting, and celebrating innovators throughout the city. This type of investment and reinvestment into the ecosystem will help propel Chicago forward as critical resources are distributed to groups working to advance and assist those in need.

This kind of work simply cannot be done without proper funding. The ecosystem's leaders must devote ample resources into programs, initiatives, and ventures in order to advance the city's global position.

5. Funders Reinvest

While the venture capital scene in Chicago has changed significantly over the last twenty years, there is still work to be done to ensure that capital remains available for budding entrepreneurs. Venture capital and private equity firms need to commit to having a diverse, Chicago-based portfolio, and the city needs to be patient enough to recognize that the gap in venture funds compared to other regions will eventually close as funding cycles yield successful returns over time.

Kevin Willer's firm, Chicago Ventures, launched in 2013 with a focus on tackling this issue of a lack of startup resources in the city. "When we started, we realized there wasn't as much capital here, and there were a lot of startups," says Kevin. "It is taking a lot longer to come to fruition than we thought." Six years later, the fund has grown. However, the capital needs of the region may have been greater than initially expected.

John Flavin, CFO of Endotronix, Inc. and former head of the Polsky Center, discusses the state of early-stage capital in Chicago: "Money is being made here, so more local funds are putting money into early stage investments. People have made money in the markets, and they are ready to make some riskier bets." There is a strong need to continue to reinvest into the ecosystem, bringing even more capital investment for early-stage companies. As the lack of early-stage capital begins to shrink, the barriers to growth for startups in the ecosystem will shrink as well.

Venture firms in Silicon Valley amass an incredible amount of funds, some of whose fundraising efforts target billions of dollars. For the mere mortals in Chicago, the calculated risk-takers, these astronomical figures are simply out of the question today. Mike Gamson, however, is optimistic about the future of Chicago's investment capabilities. To him, it's a question of economics and patience. He says, "Chicago actually produces solid venture returns, better than most markets. But it takes time to develop these funds. A fund could start at $25 million, then the next one's at $50 million, the next one's at $80 million, then $140 million, and then $200 million. So, if it takes about a year to raise a fund and three years to spend it, you have a four-year cycle for fund growth."

This four-year cycle inherently makes the funding and investments into an ecosystem a long-term bet. It is important to keep this broad, multi-year view of Chicago's venture capital scene in mind, as the proliferation of a globally recognized hub for innovation doesn't just happen overnight; it takes years, if not decades, of concerted effort. In the meantime, while fundraising numbers gradually climb among firms, the city can look at successful exits and initial public offerings as metrics for continued success among these investments being made.

Kristi Ross is one of many innovators who can point to a successful exit as proof that the investments made in the city are being put to good use. As CFO of thinkorswim, she played a key role in the company's acquisition by TD Ameritrade for $606 million in 2009. Now Co-CEO of the online financial network tastytrade, she knows that there is much ground for the city to cover in terms of cultivating investment dollars. "I don't think there will ever be a time when there is too much capital. I think the important thing is to get more venture capital firms with additional areas of expertise to Chicago." Kristi agrees that the best way to encourage capital to come to Chicago is to highlight the work that is being done by entrepreneurs, and there is a secondary role for them to play in advancing the ecosystem as well.

6. Entrepreneurs Give Back

There is a cycle of entrepreneurship in Chicago that needs to be maintained and supported for the ecosystem to grow. This cycle involves both young, first-time entrepreneurs, as well as seasoned startup veterans. While some of the most famous innovators and inventors are portrayed as solo creators, tirelessly crafting away in garages before revealing a world-changing product or service, the truth is that innovation is a team sport. No one creates a billion-dollar unicorn all by themselves. Of course, it takes a special kind of person to accomplish such impressive feats, but nevertheless, these people build successful ventures largely because of support from mentors, teachers, investors, employees, and other peer entrepreneurs. For Chicago to continue to thrive, the ecosystem needs to be continuously encouraging and incentivizing these supporters to provide guidance, advice, and capital to budding entrepreneurs.

The value of humility is crucial for Chicagoans. Successful entrepreneurs recognize that part of their role is to pay back some of the dividends they received from other members and groups within the innovation ecosystem. Caralynn Nowinski Collens is one such person. As Board Chair for digital manufacturing incubator MxD, Caralynn sees firsthand the culture that exists among these founders. "There is a 'pay it forward' attitude here that was certainly indoctrinated in me. There were so many people who helped me for free, and now there are so many people whom I can help."

As more organizations in Chicago grow and even go public, they bring with them an influx of capital into the innovation and entrepreneurial ecosystem. The way that this capital is reinvested into the region can be massively impactful. Recently, venture capital firms in Chicago founded by successful entrepreneurs like Brad Keywell, Eric Lefkofsky, Sam Yagan, or J.B. Pritzker have begun to invest more and more in early-stage companies.

Chicago's business community has an opportunity to leverage the great successes of local entrepreneurs of the last twenty years. Matt McCall says, "There are twenty-something management teams that have grown to a billion dollars. And those become angel investors, mentors, and everything else." The cycle of going from supported to supporter continues along as people reinvest time, energy, and capital into the city. Matt goes on to say, "We're now in the fourth generation of successful entrepreneurs. There are so many people who have been successful here, and then they turn around and religiously give back to the community."

That is the recipe for Chicago's growth. These entrepreneurs now have the means to give back to the city where they have been able to succeed, and they must do so in order to position the city as a global leader. The other key role they must play is becoming the faces of success for the city, because Chicago can't improve its global standing without some serious marketing efforts.

7. Everyone Tells Chicago's Story

"We might be the worst city at branding. We allow others to brand us with violence and gun issues. Who's going to rebrand us?"

Jai Shekhawat, Founder of Chicago-based Fieldglass

While humility is one of the key strengths of innovators in the city, there is a drawback to being overly humble when trying to prove one's worth in a competitive setting. Attracting talent, venture dollars, and corporate relocations takes a strong, almost boastful voice to call attention to a city's assets and capabilities. Despite numerous innovative businesses disrupting industries in Chicago, these stories are not given enough attention nationwide. So often when discussing Chicago, the conversation turns to safety or difficulties with government and finances.

There is an opportunity to change the narrative of the city towards one that accurately portrays the potential that Chicago has, and the success that has cultivated here. Rebranding Chicago as a city of innovation will be key in attracting the resources needed for new organizations to grow. Chris Gladwin says, "There needs to be more awareness both internally and externally of what is already here. Messaging and branding are a big part of this."

Bolstering Chicago's marketing efforts isn't just for the headlines; it has tangible effects on the region. It is the same reason why the property values of Silicon Valley have increased so drastically as their tech community has grown; people want to go where the money is. Andrea Zopp, CEO of World Business Chicago, contends, "Our biggest challenge is that people don't really know what we have here." Without telling people, how will they know? But whose role is it to market Chicago?

For Jai Shekhawat, "it is many people's role to tell the story of Chicago. It's the state at one level, the city at another, and the business community at a third." There are organizations like World Business Chicago that are highlighting the city's successes on the national stage. Along with the mayor, World Business Chicago works across the country and the world to shine a spotlight on all the innovative work that is happening in Chicago.

Andrea Zopp says, "I'm always blown away by the things we've made here. Cleversafe, Braintree, Fieldglass, they are all billion-dollar companies. People tend to forget all the innovation that has happened here." Andrea has worked countless hours with Mayors Rahm Emanuel and Lori Lightfoot to get Chicago on the national stage. Many agree that one of the key roles of the mayor is to shine a spotlight on Chicago. Hardik Bhatt notes, "The mayor needs to be the biggest salesperson of the city. And not just locally, but outside the city as well."

As one organization shines, it brings a spotlight onto the city, illuminating the rest of the ecosystem. A successful exit or IPO from a Chicago company pours more capital into the region, which can again be used to both build businesses and impact the community simultaneously. Sam Yagan puts it well as he describes, "It is a sort of rising tide lifts all ships mentality. I will help them out, and in turn they will help the ecosystem."

Chris Gladwin

CEO & Co-founder, Ocient

Founder & Former CEO, Cleversafe

Favorite Innovation:

Ultra

Ultra, or "the Ultra Secret," refers to the British military intelligence system for intercepting and interpreting wartime signals by breaking encrypted enemy radio and teleprinter communications.

"It was where computing was created."

Fun Fact:

When Chris Gladwin sold Cleversafe to IBM in 2015, eighty of his staffers became instant millionaires.

A Rising Tide Lifts All Ships

As one Chicago-based company or industry grows, the entire ecosystem is elevated. In order to maintain the same values-driven, collaborative culture of innovation that has been fostered, cross-industry collaboration throughout the region must be at the heart of the growth strategy. This doesn't happen by accident, and the more that leaders can draw attention to success stories of the past, the more they can inspire future ones as well.

This ideal is exemplified by the splash and ripple effect that Groupon has had in the Chicago innovation ecosystem. Groupon's record-breaking growth combined with their resistance to a lofty acquisition offer facilitated an unprecedented level of media awareness, entrepreneurial interest, and internal motivation to the Chicago innovation ecosystem. Kevin Willer, despite his work with the Google Chicago office, agrees that Groupon and Google not getting together was hugely important. "If they had been consumed by a bigger company, it would have been over. It was a huge win when Groupon went public. At that point, the *Wall Street Journal* and *New York Times* called up and asked, 'Where is Groupon? They must be in Silicon Valley. But wait, it's in Chicago?! What else is happening in Chicago?'"

The media attention that Groupon's IPO brought to Chicago showcased the immense power that one company's success can have on the entire city's reputation and awareness. In fact, in addition to several national publications writing about the company, *The Atlantic* did a focused piece entitled, "Chicago's Tech Scene After the Groupon IPO," where they came and met with entrepreneurs across the city. They say that the money generated by Groupon's IPO pumped "excitement and seed funding into Chicago's startup scene." This one success became a catalyst for national media attention focused on Chicago, which in turn facilitated more capital investment.

In a 2018 article in *Forbes*, entitled "Why Top VCs from Outside the Midwest Want In," they note that "Between 2016 and today, coastal firms have invested in Midwest startups 5.5 times more than they did during the previous three years." This is a direct result of a growing entrepreneurial community, and strong evidence of the positive feedback loop associated with communal reinvestment. Following this logic, the more that organizations can do to share their stories, the better impact they can drive. This is the goal of groups like Chicago Innovation and programs like the Momentum Awards. As Michael Krauss notes, "Awards programs like the Chicago Innovation Awards catalyze the community by focusing us around innovative organizations."

Chicago has a slew of premier awards that recognize the most innovative and successful organizations in the city. 1871 has the Momentum Awards, which celebrate the best digital technology companies. mHUB and MxD have the Fourth Revolution Awards, which celebrate leadership in innovation and manufacturing. Chicago Innovation has the Chicago Innovation Awards, which celebrate the most innovative new products, services, and organizations in the Chicago region. Chicago is even home to the James Beard Awards, celebrating the best chefs and restaurants in the country. Each of these awards creates an atmosphere of celebration and awareness building in the city.

As Marc Shiffman says, "Ultimately you need people who can recognize what has been done here and showcase that for the next group of people coming through." The successes are here, but they just need to be supported by the rest of the ecosystem, talked about, and announced. Broadcasting a company's successes not only supports the organization and its employees, but it supports the entire ecosystem.

Sustaining the Ecosystem Is a Team Sport

Chicago has evolved significantly over the past few decades to get where it is today. This growth is just the beginning. In order to ensure that the ecosystem continues to grow, each pillar will have its own unique role to play, as well as collective roles to work on together. Large corporations can provide capital to or partner with startups, who are both lifted up by a supportive government that brings people together. Nonprofits and talent creators are beginning to recognize the vital importance of collaborating, as venture funds and entrepreneurs see the need to continuously grow and reinvest into the city that brought them the success they have seen to date. All the while, each innovator, leader, and community member has the opportunity to celebrate the successes of the city to bring the entire ecosystem to new heights.

Chris Gladwin breaks it down into simple terms: "You can get lucky as an individual or a company, but a region doesn't get lucky. You have to have the goods. We have the goods: talent, capital, and grit. I think Chicago will continue to advance in its relative position because it should, and because we want it to."

CHAPTER

10 INNOVATION IS FOR EVERYONE

CHAPTER 10: INNOVATION IS FOR EVERYONE

Up until this point, the discussion around the Chicago innovation ecosystem has been largely positive. Identifying the assets and capabilities of the region allows for a discussion of how the culture of today came to fruition. In truth, it would be disingenuous to suggest that Chicago is a perfect place with only positive attributes to discuss. Chicago is not a haven. Like any other city, it is not free from challenges, and the citizens of Chicago are not blind to the work that needs to be done.

There are socioeconomic disparities, which pose a threat to the growth of the city. Unfortunately, these are the headlines that often guide the conversation around Chicago, which is a primary reason for the need to celebrate the positive aspects of the ecosystem that has been built. Nevertheless, one cannot solely discuss the positive without acknowledging the negative. These are critical obstacles that need to be prioritized among everything else, if the business community and city at large is going to reach its aspirational goals.

Chicago has not had a comprehensive land use strategy since 1966, meaning that decisions around the location of new construction have historically been left to the choice of developers. As a consequence, the northern, lakefront and downtown neighborhoods of the city have been heavily developed while communities on the South and West Sides have been largely neglected. In her December 2019 speech to the Economic Club of Chicago, Mayor Lori Lightfoot addressed this issue head on: "Income inequality has become staggeringly more pronounced over the past fifty years, with particular impact on our South and West Sides."

The Chicago innovation ecosystem does not yet include the entire city. Those who can participate in the ecosystem are living in a time of relative prosperity. As the community continues to grow each year in terms of number of people impacted, number of businesses successfully launched, and dollars earned, it needs to include these historically overlooked areas of the city. As Harper Reed, former CTO of Threadless and Obama for America, views the situation, "There's always some corridor of people who are not included. Chicago is very big, both geographically and population-wise, and you have a lot of folks who are typically not paid attention to."

In order to bring mutual prosperity to people throughout the entire city, Chicagoans need to collaborate on a scale not seen before. In truth, Chicago has been a tale of two cities, in which the upper and lower classes experience life very differently. Maria Wynne, CEO of Leadership Greater Chicago, underpins the severity of the situation: "We are among the most segregated cities in the United States. The issues that are most challenging are the issues that are brought about by the divides, both racially and socioeconomically." For the city to accelerate its growth trajectory, there has to be a stronger effort to bring more people into the fold. "By bringing together the two cities in Chicago, we will find the best solutions," agrees Sandee Kastrul.

An inclusive community is a more innovative community, and everyone benefits from growing the ecosystem in an equitable fashion. This can be done through initiatives focused on recruiting more effective mentors, upskilling and reskilling the workforce, building community, and supporting neighborhoods.

Becoming a More Inclusive City

For many years, the focus in Chicago has been to support the areas of the city that are already growing. However, as the ecosystem matures, it is important to ensure that the whole city is developing, not just the wealthier areas. Hedy Ratner notes that there are more programs and people focused on supporting the mission of making innovation and entrepreneurship accessible than ever before. "Now you see major foundations making a commitment to economic and community development across the city."

The city is in a period of waking up. Sandee Kastrul is a prime example of an innovator who has been a major contributor to inclusive efforts of the city. Her nonprofit, i.c.stars, has been helping people from historically overlooked areas build skills in technology, often helping them increase their salaries by double or more. She explains, "There are lots of ways you can work with underserved folks in our community, but we have a lot of work to do about inclusion. There is a big digital divide around giving access to people across the city."

Andrea Zopp also recognizes the challenges associated with the disconnected nature of talent in Chicago. As CEO of the Chicago Urban League, she led community-focused programs and fostered connections to help people find jobs, secure affordable housing, enhance their educational experiences, and grow their businesses. She explains the need to help young people see available pathways for opportunity: "We need to actively recruit students of color to come here and work. But you've got to get them into the engineering programs first." We need to not only invite a diverse population of working professionals to sit at the table, but support education from a young age to ensure that the pipeline of future innovators is filled.

The city is poised for success if it can come together to support all of Chicago. Historically, however, there hasn't been enough support for unifying and including the underserved areas of the city. Chicago's overall population is fairly evenly divided: according to the 2010 U.S. Census, the city's racial breakdown is 32.7 percent white, 30.5 percent black, 29 percent Hispanic, and 6.2 percent Asian. However, the communities and ecosystems within Chicago are highly segregated.

Most of Chicago's white population lives in the northern neighborhoods, and most of the non-white population lives in the west and south of the city. As Jai Shekhawat describes, "We've found a way to segregate the hell out of this place. Whose fingerprints are on that one? No one's and everyone's." Now, it is everyone's problem to solve. It's critical to note that this problem is not unique to Chicago; many large cities worldwide face similar issues of subregional disparity. This issue must be addressed for any progress to be made in the next decade.

With more diverse perspectives, innovation will occur at a quicker and more successful rate. It is better for everyone to bring more people into the conversation. According to *Forbes' Global Diversity and Inclusion Report*, diversity is a key driver of innovation. In fact, *Forbes* conducted a study that found 85 percent of senior executives agree that a diverse workforce stimulates innovation. Kristi Ross of tastytrade agrees, "A thriving innovation ecosystem begins with diversity. Diversity of thought along with collaboration leads to innovation." Without diversity of thought and experience, innovation and success will plateau in Chicago.

Diversity is a critical component of success on a global scale for organizations. Harper Reed puts it in simple terms: "If you're building a product for everyone, your team needs to look like everyone." It is crucial for companies that want to attract and retain top talent, and executives are recognizing now more than ever that diverse perspectives, backgrounds, and experiences play a critical role in the success of the organization.

As the idea of diversity within an organization is extrapolated to the size of an entire city, it is clear why Chicago needs to be more inclusive. As senior executives across the country recognize that diversity is important, those in Chicago should recognize the talent that already exists here. But people who have been historically excluded from the conversation face additional barriers, including not being aware they have a seat at the table.

You Can't Be What You Can't See

"My favorite seven-year-old said, 'the hope needs you,' and I think about it all the time. The future of our innovation ecosystem in Chicago is about hope."

Sandee Kastrul, CEO of i.c.stars

Chicagoans are hopeful about the city's ability to support underrepresented neighborhoods and populations. There is a lot to be hopeful about. However, for Chicago's young future innovators to thrive, they will need role models and mentors who look like them. This is how to truly communicate to young people that they can be whomever they want to be when they grow up.

In a study completed by AARP, 83 percent of working adults stated that mentorships benefited their career, and 81 percent of older adults are willing to mentor the next generation. However, for the most part, finding a mentor is more difficult for people from typically underrepresented communities. This is where the vowels of "The C.H.I.C.A.G.O. Way" come into play: Inclusion, Altruism, and Openness. Programs geared toward mentoring and helping others come naturally for a community that holds these values dear; the key focus needs to be making sure those programs are equitably targeting all types of communities.

Starting at a young age, nonprofits like Girls in the Game do so much to connect young girls with mentors across Chicago's diverse neighborhoods. A past Chicago Innovation Award winner,

Girls in the Game is an after-school program that helps young women find their voice, discover their strengths, and lead with confidence through sports, health and leadership programs. In this program, younger and older girls are paired, creating leadership opportunities and role models to inspire future leaders.

MENTOR Illinois is another organization that promotes mentorships across the entire city. This organization has developed national best practices for mentoring, and has shared them with over four hundred organizations that serve fifty-five thousand young people across the state. They also have played an important role in increasing public awareness of the value of mentorships in healthy youth development, violence prevention, academic achievement, and workforce readiness.

From a young age, children in Chicago have the opportunity to connect with a number of different organizations to learn important skills like coding, invention, and problem solving. The Chicago Student Invention Convention empowers teachers across the city in forty-five schools, youth centers, and library branches to teach an innovation curriculum to thirty-five hundred students across the state, 61 percent of whom are girls and 80 percent of whom come from low-income families. Sonia Torres, a fourth-grade teacher at Jungman Elementary School whose students won top prize at the statewide competition, says: "Students are naturally good thinkers. They are naturally creative. A program like this allows them to master and share their skills." These students are representative of the state and the city, with a very diverse racial, socioeconomic, and gender breakdown.

After School Matters is another nonprofit organization that provides after-school and summer program opportunities to nearly nineteen thousand Chicago high school teens each year. In a similar spirit, Chicago Youth Centers focuses on providing access to high-quality youth development programs for children living in Chicago's various communities, serving 1,400 youth and 700 families in 7 centers and several partner sites.

As young students get older, there are also opportunities to learn new skills and be inspired to lead. Future Founders immerses youth in experiences that inspire and empower them to create their own opportunities. They have served over thirty-five thousand youth, developing the next generation of business leaders and entrepreneurs.

But young people aren't the only ones that benefit from mentoring. While the impact on kids can be massive in terms of understanding what future possibilities are available to them, there are adults across the region who need various levels of support in order to become valued members of the ecosystem. Chicago needs to get people involved across age ranges and across neighborhoods to maximize the benefits from the diverse perspectives across the city. There is a key need to ensure that people have the tools to succeed, and a major way to do this is through mentorship and education.

Today, many organizations like 1871, Chicago Innovation, and ARA each have a female-focused mentoring program to help women navigate the difficulties of starting their own businesses. WiSTEM is a twelve-week program run by 1871 that helps early-stage female founders develop, launch, and grow tech businesses faster. Chicago Innovation's Women Mentoring Co-op, launched in 2015, focuses on female innovators both starting their own companies and attempting to break glass ceilings and rise through corporate ranks. ARA, which stands for Attract, Retain, and Advance Women in Technology, has grown since its launch in 2012, and now shares Chicago-based values of mentorship and innovation with seven cities across the country.

The Chicago Network, headed up by Kate Bensen, is another organization focused on empowering women to lead. This group of five hundred female leaders across industries serves as a community for young women looking to grow and learn. They recognize that people can't be what they can't see, and they broadcast female successes through "HerStories," stories from Chicago women making change.

It is because of organizations like these that Chicago boasts the highest concentration of female-led startups in the country. However, that number is only 34 percent; there is still work to be done to continue to grow equitably.

Mentorship is not the only way to ensure that young innovators and entrepreneurs from across the city can see potential growth opportunities. Increasing representation on boards is another way that an organization can broadcast its commitment to supporting inclusion and diversity, while at the same time bringing in new, highly effective board members. Today's boards, both corporate and nonprofit, still have a lot of work to do in terms of bringing on more women and people of color. Increasing the diversity of boards benefits all, and many are becoming more and more aware of this truth. The trouble for some is simply taking the leap and committing to change.

People like Mike Gamson recognize that a personal commitment to a cause sometimes means putting themselves on the line. "Let's say you believe that it's important that women and men should get equal amount of representation on boards. If you believe that, and you are doing nothing about it, I would say that you don't really care about it." Systematic change doesn't just happen on its own, and if Chicago is going to grow to become a global leader, it's going to need to leverage the insights from every type of person. Mike, possibly thanks to his experience as an executive at LinkedIn, knows how crucial diverse talent can be for an organization. He took action to start building the community he wants to see. "I called a bunch of CEOs whose boards I was on that were all male, and I said, 'I'm going to leave if you don't add some women.' I went down the list, and there are now women on all those boards."

Getting more diversity into boardrooms creates a sense of possibility for those looking upwards. Once people begin to see what is possible for them, inspiration kicks in. These leaders bring a unique perspective to the table, but they also need to bring significant functional expertise. Leadership, vision, and confidence might come naturally to many people at the top, but programming, finance, and engineering do not; these are learned skills that need to be taught and developed. To advance the innovation ecosystem equitably, programs teaching these specific, high-level skills need to be accessible for all types of people interested in learning.

Upskill and Reskill the Workforce

There is a huge opportunity to train talent across Chicago's diverse neighborhoods in order to give a stronger voice to a new crop of employees. For Harper Reed, this is one of the city's greatest assets: "Chicago is great because you have such a talented, diverse population to hire from." There are many organizations and nonprofits that work to broaden Chicago's talent pool, and are doing so in a way that ensures innovation is truly for everyone.

Sandee Kastrul has been supporting Chicago's underserved population through workforce development and talent creation since day one. She says, "We have a lot of work to do in terms of inclusion. In my world of workforce development and technology education, there are more of us involved in this space than ever. But just twenty years ago, there weren't many." Sandee has been a driving force for bringing technology education programs to these communities. Though her journey isn't finished yet, she's finally seeing peer groups getting involved.

As companies channel their corporate social responsibility divisions and look outward to make an impact, many have found workforce development and training programs to be an extremely powerful way to contribute to the ecosystem. In 2016, both Accenture and Apple collaborated with the City Colleges of Chicago to launch a program to support the city's youth. In this program, the schools train digital apprentices who upon graduating will have a job ready for them at Accenture. Apple also launched an initiative called "Everyone Can Code" to help young students across the country learn to code and prepare for the workforce. City Colleges of Chicago is collaborating with Apple to bring coding to Chicago's nearly five hundred thousand students through a citywide expansion.

Focused on college-aged students, One Million Degrees targets the one-in-four Illinois community college students who are not on track to graduate with a degree within three years. From tutors and coaches to financial assistance and professional development, this organization supports highly motivated college students who need some wraparound support to help them succeed. Coding Dojo is another organization that is providing skills-based training to serve the needs in today's changing economy. Their thousands of alumni work at organizations like Google, Amazon, Facebook, and IBM.

There are also groups that train and support currently unemployed people in Chicago to ensure their success going forward. Sandee Kastrul's group i.c.stars, Skills for Chicagoland's Future, Cara, StreetWise, and more are training and empowering underserved, underrepresented, but unbeaten communities whose ambition and hard work allow them to rise through the ranks of many organizations. Their work brings new faces to the table, new voices to the conversation, and new dimensions to the community.

Providing Opportunities for Entrepreneurs

Incubators, accelerators, and coworking spaces have demonstrated a unique capacity to support a variety of specific communities, and showcase that anyone can be a successful entrepreneur. Bunker Labs, run by Todd Connor, allows veterans and military spouses access to entrepreneurial programs and resources online, educational opportunities, and a thriving network of entrepreneurs, all free of charge.

Typical programs geared toward veterans focus on traditional forms of employment, but there are far fewer resources for veteran entrepreneurs. Correspondingly, 25 percent of veterans are interested in starting a business, but only 4.5 percent pursue their entrepreneurial dreams. Since launching in 2015 in Chicago, Bunker Labs has grown across the country and currently hosts over twenty chapters nationwide.

EvolveHer is one of several coworking spaces that focuses on empowering a community of women to lead, learn, and grow. They feature a creative workspace designed to support women leading organizations through community building and collaboration. Female leaders empower women by sharing best practices and advice that helped them navigate the unique challenges that female entrepreneurs face. EvolveHer broke new ground in 2018 with the launch of their accelerator space, but there have been women laying the foundation for years so that places like this could exist today.

The Women's Business Development Center (WBDC), founded by Hedy Ratner and Carol Dougal, has been advocating for and supporting women and minorities since its founding in 1986. At a time when women and minority entrepreneurs simply could not get the resources to start their businesses, the WBDC stepped in. Hedy shares her early work: "We worked with financial institutions to provide technical assistance to make the women and minority-owned businesses bank-loan ready, and we also did direct loans to women-owned businesses that the banks wouldn't touch because they were considered high risk." Hedy Ratner understood that in order to support people who needed help most, she needed to take on some risk herself.

She took that step to open the door for women and minority business to propel them forward, and the impact is still felt today.

Linda Darragh notes, "The Women's Business Development Center has done an amazing job in pulling the women together."

It is important to have these types of organizations whose sole focus is advocating and supporting the various communities that make up a city. They keep diversity and inclusion top of mind, and assure that every type of person is represented. These are the groups that will make sure growth is equitable and inclusive. As such, they require support. A few more examples of these groups are:

The Center on Halsted is the largest LGBTQ community center in the Midwest with over one thousand people walking through its doors each day. They have transformed Chicago's North Side by helping create a neighborhood and safe space for the LGBTQ community. The Center on Halsted also serves as an incubator for smaller nonprofit LGBTQ organizations. They provide operational support, space, and resources for organizations that may otherwise find it difficult to interact and grow.

Blue1647 is an entrepreneurship and technology innovation center focused on education and workforce development in Chicago's South Side. They support the ecosystem by enabling women, young Latinas, and entrepreneurs to excel in technology and leadership. Their programs have facilitated inclusion across Chicago for people of all ages.

The Illinois Hispanic Chamber of Commerce is a community of business owners, entrepreneurs, and professionals committed to empowering individuals through economic growth. This organization engages entrepreneurs through community advocacy, networking, and one-on-one training designed to help leaders become agents of change. A recent partnership with 1871 led to the creation of Latinx, a three-month business incubation program for Chamber-member startups.

The Chicago Urban League is focused on promoting strong, sustainable communities in order to support economic, educational, and social progress for African Americans. They offer a variety of programs aimed at student and workforce development, entrepreneurship and innovation, housing and financial empowerment, and leadership development.

The Chicago Inventors Organization provides affordable, credible resources to independent inventors. This serves as a community group as well as a resource provider to inventors who might not have other support at their disposal.

Groups like these make a tremendous impact in establishing a future-focused, inclusive culture in a region. They are a critical model for driving support to communities that need it most. However, in order to get to the next level, bridges need to be created between these proliferating communities and the rest of the ecosystem. It's a group effort, after all, and the innovation ecosystem needs to come together as one.

Opening Doors and Being an Ally

"Frankly, I think opening a door is the most powerful act of inclusion that you can possibly do."

Mike Gamson, CEO, Relativity

Opening a door and forging an introduction can lead to powerful outcomes. So many of today's CEOs, founders, and community leaders were able to make a significant career jump or take hold of an amazing opportunity because of a single introduction, phone call, or meeting. On the scale of privilege and fortune, there are "silver spooners" that have found themselves in the right place, time, and economic situation for most of their lives. Not to say they haven't worked hard and earned their achievements, but these types of people tend to find opportunities presented more frequently and often within reach.

For people on the opposite side of the spectrum, they face barriers to entry at every turn. These are the types of people for whom a values-driven and inclusive community needs to open doors. Mike Gamson has a simple approach to making conscious decisions to open doors for people. "Let's say I get X number of inbounds per week of entrepreneurs in the city that are asking for my time for something. I make a conscious decision to say 'yes' more to the groups who I know are probably getting more 'nos.'"

Simple actions like taking meetings and answering calls may take up five minutes to an hour of someone's time, but in doing so they can make a monumental impact. Not only does it build a relationship, it is also a signal of trust in the people being introduced. In an act as simple as an email introduction, Mike can signal to both parties, "I support you." It is the true embodiment

John Flavin

CFO, Endotronix, Inc.

Former Head of the Polsky Center for Entrepreneurship and Innovation at the University of Chicago

Fun Fact:

John has completed numerous public and private capital financings totaling over $275 million including two NASDAQ IPOs, and has raised over $135 million in philanthropic and corporate funding to support university technology commercialization and venture start-up activities.

of being an ally. It harkens back to the values of altruism and openness.

Linda Darragh agrees that there is an aspect of this that is Chicago-centric: the desire to share and support one another. She says, "Most times, everyone will take a call or meet with someone; they'll fit it into their schedule. People will make referrals, and that's how the networks continue to grow." Growing a network isn't just about meeting people who will help a person's organization or advance their agenda. It means investing time to help others in the community, not because it might yield a personal return, but in order to make a net positive for the ecosystem as a whole.

A collective of small additions adds up to an immense sum. With the entire city supporting one another, better economic outcomes can occur for everyone, from the more affluent neighborhoods down to those that need more support.

Not everyone is a networking fiend with over five hundred contacts on LinkedIn and a drawer full of business cards or phone numbers written on cocktail napkins. But that doesn't mean there aren't other ways to open doors for people and be an ally in some way. John Flavin says, "I think giving back to the city is critical. Everybody has their own ways of thinking about how they reinvest or volunteer." Giving back, for many successful innovators in Chicago, is often sitting on boards and mentoring the next generation.

For people like Mike Gamson, being a door opener means forging introductions and investing time, effort, and real dollars into sprouting entrepreneurs. A great example of this is Mike's relationship with a local tech startup that helps people run employee resource groups (ERGs). The founder, an African American woman, had reached out to Mike during a time when he was avoiding investments and focusing on his new role as the CEO of Relativity. Despite not looking for investing opportunities, Mike took the meeting because of his decision that "if you are an African American female founder in the city trying to get a meeting, you face a harder path to a 'yes' almost all of the time. That's why I make a point of saying 'yes' more often. I may not be your investor, but I know so many people who can help you." He recognized a need and an opportunity where he could provide a significant impact.

As the city seeks to develop a globally leading community and culture surrounding innovation, this spirit for and commitment to inclusion, opening doors, and giving back to the ecosystem is more important than ever. Today's successful Chicago entrepreneurs built their ventures from the ground up with the support of other innovators. These people who have seen the growth of the ecosystem understand the necessity to give back and support the next generation of leaders across the entire city.

Supporting the Neighborhoods

In addition to supporting innovators on an individual level, there are many groups providing resources to bolster the economies of neighborhoods on the South and West Sides. As an example, the city government currently has particular interest in economic development initiatives in neighborhoods like Austin, where 35 percent of people depend on public assistance, or Roseland, where the unemployment rate is 26 percent.

Some companies are getting involved in this strategy through their recruitment, as well as rethinking their entire infrastructure to be more focused on the community. Wintrust is one of those organizations, and has branded itself as "Chicago's Bank" for good reason. They aim to bring value to the city across Chicago's diverse neighborhoods by focusing on the community.

Ed Wehmer, Founder and CEO of Wintrust Financial, celebrates the diversity of his customers' communities through regular programs and events. "Every month we'll have an event down at the Wintrust Grand Banking Hall. We celebrate Black History Month, we celebrate veterans, we celebrate the Hispanic Chamber." For Ed, it's not just about celebrating, it's about learning from people of different backgrounds and perspectives too. "I learn so much sitting there and listening to the real needs of the community. It helps me figure out how to take care of everyone so we can be Chicago's bank." It makes logical sense that the more closely connected an organization is with its surrounding community, the better it can serve the needs of its customers. It just so happens to also be the right thing to do.

Wintrust also supports Chicagoans across the city through their involvement with Chicago Innovation as the Presenting Sponsor of the Chicago Neighborhood Awards, which shine a spotlight on organizations innovating with a localized impact in their neighborhoods. The awards serve to legitimize people that might not have considered themselves innovative because of the localized scale of their work, as well as draw attention to the need for problem-solving innovations within these neighborhood areas. Many of these award recipients innovate through social good for particular communities, such as the Chicago Neighborhood Initiatives' Pullman Revitalization Project. Within the Pullman neighborhood, they have recruited national and local businesses, partnered with residential and commercial developers to renovate or build multifamily and single-family housing, and attracted retail amenities to accommodate the associated growing market need. Through this initiative, they have created fifteen hundred new jobs, and generated $350 million of investment into Pullman. As a result, violent crime in this neighborhood is down 52 percent since the project began, and the number of six-figure households has increased by 58 percent.

Other organizations create solutions for their neighborhoods that are smaller in scale, but maintain similar potentials for impact. Boombox is an example of this in action. They have created pop-up storefronts constructed from upcycled shipping containers, and provide micro-retail spaces for new entrepreneurs that lack the capital to afford their own retail presence. Their locations anchor neighborhood commercial corridors across Chicago, ranging from vacant land sites to public plazas that provide a bridge between startup and storefront for small retail businesses in Chicago's neighborhoods.

On the government side, there are lots of initiatives focused on bringing some of the economic prosperity felt on the North Side of the city into the South and West Sides. Holly Copeland, former Deputy Director for the Illinois State Office of Entrepreneurship, Innovation, and Technology, notes that "government has a role to play in creating the foundation, and they have the convening power to bring all the right parties together." The most recent major initiative to make this happen is Mayor Lori Lightfoot's INVEST South/West Plan.

According to the Mayor, "The city will channel more than $750 million over the next three years in order to attract private capital, respond to changing commercial trends, and enrich local culture." The goal of this initiative is to reactivate neighborhoods that have been focal points of commerce and activity in the southern and western parts of the city, encouraging the development of shopping centers, services, transportation, public spaces, and improved quality-of-life amenities for residents. However, it is not just the government that will be involved in supporting the ten neighborhoods receiving funding through this initiative.

The plan will convene government, businesses, philanthropic organizations, and community groups to make coordinated investments and drive inclusive, measurable growth throughout each of the ten neighborhoods. INVEST South/West will leverage $250 million in business development infrastructure that already exists from the Neighborhood Opportunity Fund and the Small Business Improvement Fund in order to ensure that business and government spending are aligned with the purpose of bolstering the vitality of these areas.

If the program comes to fruition as promised, it will serve as a quintessential model for how an innovation ecosystem can and should function. It shines a spotlight on Mayor Lightfoot's efforts to ensure that the prosperity experienced in Chicago is shared throughout the city.

The outlook for Chicago is bright. There is a flourishing ecosystem with the capacity to grow equitably and maintain the intrinsic values that make it unique such as inclusion, altruism and openness. However, without a conscious focus on including the entire city within the Chicago innovation ecosystem, the city will never grow to reach its true potential. There is an opportunity to grow the city upwards as well as outwards, and to leverage the diverse perspectives of all of Chicago's great innovators and entrepreneurs. If this can be achieved, the only limiting factor for how far the ecosystem can grow is the extent of its citizens' imaginations.

CHAPTER
11
BOLD VISIONS

CHAPTER 11: BOLD VISIONS

It is a spring evening in 1970. It's a little cloudy atop the tallest building in the world, the 110th floor of the Sears Tower. The nighttime glow of the Chicago electric grid can be seen in every direction. All at once, the clouds begin to clear and, unnaturally, just as quickly reappear. Thousands of headlights below begin moving faster into a connected blur. Time is speeding up.

In a fifty-year time-lapse, the city seems to build itself up gradually as the years progress. Cranes swing, new towers poke holes in the sky and one million people quickly multiply to three million. As the clock settles on the present day, one can't help but wonder what changes the next fifty years will bring.

Do the suburbs disappear into a single, widespread megacity? Do construction projects break the coastal barrier with buildings floating on Lake Michigan, connected to the mainland by hyperloops? Does this ecosystem continually expand its boundaries like moss on a forest floor? Or does it build up higher, with new two-hundred-story skyscrapers dwarfing the now Willis Tower in their wake? And what about Chicago's relation to the world beyond; is the fate of all cities an abandonment of local identity in favor of global connectedness?

Something is lost from this bird's-eye view. While progress seems to be guided by the unstoppable tides of tomorrow, it is individual people who set the course.

They can't be seen from up here, and neither can their ambitions. They're too tiny on their own. But all this grand movement cannot happen without them. The rich innovation ecosystem seen today was built from the bold visions of past Chicagoans; innovators who imagined their own future, and proceeded to build what they saw. Today's innovators have the city's best sightlines, and they aren't looking down. They're looking up.

What do they see? What's next for a city with a history of radical reinvention and a skyrocketing reputation for innovation? Is what we see when we close our eyes anything like the world we're approaching? Let's ask the innovators.

Rewinding the Future

"All good ecosystems point to family trees."

Matt McCall, Partner at Pritzker Group Venture Capital

As was identified at the outset of this conversation, one of the primary directives for any innovation ecosystem is to facilitate the transformation of new ideas into realities. Perhaps it seems a little counterintuitive that something so complex and methodically cultivated like an innovation ecosystem does, in a sense, lay the groundwork for total unpredictability. No one knows which ideas will turn into viable innovations that will change the course of the city and beyond; even the most prolific innovators only expect a 60 percent success rate because of the unpredictable nature of innovation.

It seems risky, almost hubristic, to pontificate about what may lie decades into the future with any sense of assured inevitability. Who can really guess what tomorrow's news will be? In truth, no one.

However, lines can be drawn based on the current upward trajectory of the region. Following trends, one can make assumptions as to what is more likely than not, and rely on the preservation of today's values to ensure Chicago's business community will continue rising together. Besides, history always seems to hold some mysterious future-telling ability, doesn't it?

Theodore Roosevelt once said, "The more you know about the past, the better prepared you are for the future." This may have been the case a century ago, and though the theory likely still holds true, it's tempting to wonder how faithful it remains with almost daily advancements in technologies like artificial intelligence and quantum computing leading us into the future at breakneck speeds. The innovators think the culture will persevere. However fast today's society may venture toward distant visions of the future, one can predict a sense of where it's headed by looking at the compounding groundwork.

Just as a strong company is built upon a good idea, solid leadership, and a well-defined and practiced culture, a city relies on this same foundational formula. When the city was essentially rebuilt from scratch after the great fire of 1871, it had the opportunity to seize upon a new identity and infrastructure that has remained a cornerstone of its DNA ever since. The values of

The C.H.I.C.A.G.O. Way are ingrained in today's culture by means of the city's ancestors: immigrants, industrialists, inventors, and idealists, all coming together under a common identity.

"You saw all different kinds of people show up to rebuild the city," says Ed Wehmer, CEO of Wintrust. The city's response to the fire of 1871 stripped away the exterior to reveal the character within. And the city's response was telling. "We got completely obliterated, and we had to come together to rebuild," adds Andrea Zopp, CEO of World Business Chicago. "The fire destroyed the city and what did we do? We turned a river around!"

Diversity, shared identity, collaboration, and opportunity. Could this be a cultural formula for innovation?

After a dramatic resurgence that included Chicago's crowning as the manufacturing capital of the West, a host of world-changing inventions, the construction of the world's tallest building, and the development of the most advanced urban infrastructure of its time, it's clear that Chicago was a city of innovation before the term "innovation" became commonplace.

The rebuild isn't over. The same construction project continues over a century later. While other cities are crafting a culture out of the recent tech boom and grappling for an identity in a quickly changing landscape, Chicago has long been primed to meet this wave of new opportunity in stride.

Battle of the Brains

"We attract mission-driven people with talent; they are joining to make an impact. There is something to be said for the Midwestern culture in that regard. It is the brain and the heart together."

John Flavin, CFO, Endotronix, Inc.

Twenty years from now there's a Netflix series entitled, "The Talent Wars," found under the "culture" and "documentaries" tags. It chronicles the race among cities for specialized talent in the wake of a technological revolution. A successful series that becomes required viewing in every online and virtual-reality university, it ends thrillingly with the emergence of Chicago as the victor in the war for talent. Well, at least one of the victors. It'll be easy to look back in hindsight and see what led to this outcome.

In a theoretical war for talent, there are some basic essentials for the city armory: top universities, affordability, livability, opportunity, breadth of industry, and culture. Chicago has stacked the deck in this regard. But some would argue the city hasn't been as aggressive as it should be. There is still the pervasive issue of, as Mike Gamson put it, "tech companies not knowing the data scientists are here, and data scientists not knowing the tech companies are looking for them."

The explosion of startup culture has ushered in major shifts in the mechanics governing talent flow. Similar changes in the recruitment process for marquee sports franchises have turned the way they look for new additions to the team on its head. Teams with shiny new stadiums and major-market fan bases are picking their athletes up in hot tub-equipped limousines and their owners are making promises to be the first team to play on Mars. Meanwhile, the actual future champions are sucking down raw eggs in their garage gymnasium.

Elegant innovation labs and product lines with a sexy cultural buzz around them are great. And Chicago has some of those, but innovation isn't fueled by trends. It takes hard work that over time inspires trends and creates new value.

Chicago's "master-the-basics" mentality is well suited for the long game of building out an ecosystem sustained by an ever-flowing influx of talent. Chicago's innovators are interested in very real problems, and the city attracts talent drawn to developing very real solutions. This ecosystem doesn't need a team of Michael Jordans and LeBron Jameses, as Sam Yagan, CEO of ShopRunner, put it: "I'm sure the world's best engineers are in the Valley, but I don't need the best engineers. I need very, very good engineers." Chicago has a two-part factory for specialized talent. The first part is its universities.

If a good indicator of the future of a city is the quality of its young talent, then Chicago's horizon is glowing. Chicago is home to the number one business school in the world, the Booth School of Business at the University of Chicago, and another top-ten ranked program in the Kellogg School of Management at Northwestern University. South of Northwestern University is the Illinois Institute of Technology, where its accelerated innovation master's program and its state-of-the-art Kaplan Center for innovation brings together design majors, technologists, researchers, and business students for an interdisciplinary experience with a practical approach.

Add to the roster DePaul University, Loyola University, the University of Illinois at Chicago, the School of the Art Institute of Chicago, City Colleges, and others. Together, they power a city brimming with new talent. But the real game changer is when these university programs are connected with and absorbed into a city's innovation ecosystem.

City officials, business leaders, and academic decision makers alike are realizing that the bold visions for the city will require bold reimaginings of how a university should function. Linda Darragh, professor of Entrepreneurial Practice at the Kellogg School of Management, explains her approach to drawing lines out from the university into the business world. "We needed to have faculty with a toe in the ecosystem. Adjuncts who were venture capitalists, serial entrepreneurs, etc. We now have at least twenty-two faculty who are all part of the ecosystem."

This marriage between Chicago's universities and its network of businesses ranging from startups to corporations is one of the keys to growing talent the right way, and keeping it local. "The volume of students is so big, and the quality is so good," says Chris Gladwin, who has built skilled talent forces around his companies Cleversafe and Ocient. "If you wanted to hire one hundred thousand people, you can just do that in Chicago. In other cities, this has gotten more expensive, there is more competition, and the supply of talent has gone down as compared to the demand." While other cities become more saturated and overpopulated, Chicago maintains a capacity for growth.

Linda Darragh

Executive Director Northwestern University's Kellogg School of Management Innovation & Entrepreneurship Initiative

Fun Fact:

Having spent three decades focused on enhancing entrepreneurship in Chicago, Linda was awarded the Entrepreneurial Champion Award by 1871 in 2018.

The Magic of Proliferation

The ecosystem cannot function without a population of individuals all fighting for the same goal. In stride with Chicago's burgeoning talent pool is a proliferation of startups, nonprofits, and corporate offices, as well as ecosystem connectors like incubators, coworking spaces, maker labs, member-based organizations, and accelerator programs. In terms of increasing impact, Chicago has seen its number of nonprofits nearly double from 2010-2019.

The banner examples for the positive feedback loop of startup proliferation in Chicago are the founders of Groupon. After taking the company public in 2014, Eric Lefkofsky and Brad Keywell began two new companies: Lefkofsky launched Tempus, a medical data company, and Keywell started Uptake, a predictive analytics software maker for clients in the mining, aviation, rail, energy, retail, and construction industries. Chicago is a ripe environment for serial entrepreneurship. Innovators are continuing to build new companies and hire people by the hundreds, which bodes well for the ecosystem's economic outlook. For Brad and Eric, this doesn't end with one or two companies. The two have founded several companies large and small, such as Echo Global Logistics, MediaOcean, and Starbelly, and even started an investment firm, Lightbank that has since invested in fifty-three Chicago startups. They're a prime model for entrepreneurial proliferation within the ecosystem.

Access is key for all of this to be possible, especially for entrepreneurs. Katlin Smith, the Founder of Simple Mills, a Chicago-based company that sells snacks and baking mixes that are gluten- and GMO-free, explained to *Inc. Magazine* that quick access to partners in manufacturing, food science, and transportation logistics makes it easier to run her business. "You don't have to travel to meet partners to grow aspects of the business. If I was based on the West Coast, I would be traveling to Chicago a lot."

The city of the future is buzzing with a network of connected people, and they're not constrained to the hallways of a handful of tech giants. They're at work building their ideas into reality, across a breadth of industries and a community of access afforded by the ecosystem. And these ideas are charged with impact at a global scale.

Set the DeLorean for 2040

Chicago, Illinois. The third largest city in the United States. The cultural gem and economic giant of the Midwest. The only city to have mastered the hot dog and the hottest place in the country for corporate relocations. All of these statements only have meaning in the context of one country out of almost two hundred worldwide.

As cities compete for people and resources, they often do so with the mental confines of their national borders. In other words, thinking nationally instead of globally. But viewing a city as an innovation ecosystem inherently identifies it as a forward-thinking disruptor of the status quo. Advancing the conversation forward by a decade or two, invisible borders begin to fade and the role of the city of tomorrow as a global player comes into focus.

This two-decade lens isn't arbitrary. It harkens back to the recently formed coalition, P33, which is tasked with laying a blueprint for establishing Chicago as a global tech leader. If the city's innovation ecosystem is a large body of distinct parts, then P33 is a nervous system of sorts, sending signals out to the various organs and muscles so they all function with a unified goal. Comprised of business, nonprofit, and government leaders from every industry, the organization was developed by philanthropist and former U.S. Secretary of Commerce Penny Pritzker, tech entrepreneur Chris Gladwin, and the Commercial Club of Chicago with the ultimate goal of solidifying the city as a leading global tech hub by 2033.

One century after the Chicago World's Fair of 1933, the group hopes to once again establish the city as a North Star for innovation and technology worldwide. This doesn't happen overnight, which is why they are getting started now. "If we are really doing this well, we need to be focused ten to twenty years out," says Kevin Willer, Founder of Chicago Ventures and a founding committee member of P33. "One of the greatest things about P33 is that it's commercially driven instead of political, and it's focused on the next two decades, which is necessary." A non-governmental organization, the group isn't beholden to four-year term limits for its agenda; they are thinking at a grander scale than those in office can accomplish before re-election time.

Part of the foundational thinking of P33 is the idea that big cities are diverging, and those that succeed long term will be the ones that have the most valuable differentiators. They create value, and they capture value; the two sides of the innovation coin. The other idea is that a city needs to be globally minded. A city that isn't competing and contributing on a global stage is, by 2040, a city whose ecosystem has long since fossilized.

And what are Chicago's key differentiators? First think back to the talent piece. If an institution should look like the community it serves, and if that community is a global one, then Chicago has that box checked. As a sanctuary city for immigrants, the city welcomes top minds from across the globe. "You don't have to worry about our city policies working against you. We're progressive. We're recruiting young, diverse talent," says Andrea Zopp. Her comments are supported by the fact that Chicago is ranked number two in the U.S. for immigrant-friendly policies. Another feather in the cap for the "Second City."

Harper Reed, the former CTO for Barack Obama's re-election campaign, backs up the idea that a global performer will have global performers: "When we're looking at the country's role in innovation in the future, if we don't have an aggressive relationship with diversity and accessibility, we're lost. For example, how do you enter China? Who in Chicago can do that if we have no Chinese people? It's a big market." Reed has made a career out of predicting trends and stepping just far enough into the future to outpace his contemporaries. He has long been viewing Chicago in terms of how it is poised to behave on a global scale, and his comment above is a frank assessment of what will make an innovation ecosystem successful moving into the future.

Another key differentiator is Chicago's diverse economy. This, in combination with a growing talent pool, collaborative culture, and deep-rooted values, makes for a unique backbone that will need to be nurtured even more aggressively as Chicago moves into its next phase as a global innovation hub.

So, what is the work of a city in 2040? If a city is truly an innovation ecosystem ready for a successful future, then surely this work is already in motion. Looking at a figurative 2040 compass, there's a strong magnetic pull coming from the Chicago suburb of Lemont, about twenty-five miles southwest of downtown.

Something like an "Area 51" of the Midwest, Argonne National Laboratory is a science and engineering research lab funded in part by the United States Department of Energy and led by

UChicago Argonne, LLC. Argonne was initially formed to carry out Enrico Fermi's work on nuclear reactors as part of the Manhattan Project, and it was designated as the first national laboratory in the United States in 1946. In the post-war era, the lab designed the first power-producing nuclear reactors, and helped design the reactors used by the U.S. nuclear navy, among other similar projects. Today, the lab maintains a broad portfolio in chemical research, energy storage and renewable energy, environmental sustainability, and supercomputing.

The tech boom connected the world, and the Internet of Things movement put everything on the grid. Now, predictive analytics, machine learning, and blockchain are creating pathways to achieve previously unthinkable efficiencies, and are becoming vital tools for any company to compete. But at a place like Argonne, which exists in the today while operating squarely in the tomorrow, supercomputing is a top investment.

The lab's two primary supercomputers are housed in a twenty-five thousand square foot data center. Their names are Mira and Theta, and they're about to get a new lab partner, a $500 million associate named Aurora. This powerful new supercomputer will be the first "exascale" supercomputer capable of performing one quintillion calculations per second. The U.S. Department of Energy, which runs Argonne and seventeen other national laboratories, is investing $1.8 billion.

To put this kind of speed in context, the system will be between five and ten times quicker than the current reigning champ of supercomputers, the IBM-Nvidia mega-machine called Summit. Put in more tangible terms courtesy of *Design News*, "A person adding 1+1+1 into a hand calculator once per second, without time off to eat or sleep, would need 31.7 trillion years to do what Aurora will do in one second."

There are many other technological toys being built at Argonne, but the facility behaves something like a siloed playground of apparent science fiction. For the lab to play its part as a driver of the innovation ecosystem, it will need to spend some time getting to know its neighbors, learn how to more effectively commercialize its discoveries, and develop partnerships.

An example partnership that would be perfect for the laboratory is with P33; one of P33's four industry clusters is life and health sciences. If nurtured into a tighter symbiosis with groups like

Argonne, this industry space may hold the key to Chicago's future considering the city currently holds six hundred thousand life sciences jobs. With powerful innovative giants such as Argonne in tandem with local corporations like Exelon and nimble startups like Tempus and CancerIQ, the next step does indeed seem to lie in fostering connections and collaborations between these players.

Bold Visions for You

As we've learned, an innovation ecosystem is a complex network composed of many elements swarming and collaborating, all with a shared set of values and goals. But the key element is people coming together. This book is entitled *Rising Together,* after all.

Through conversations with the thirty-one people interviewed for this book, we heard so many insights about culture, community, the trajectory for the city, how the innovation ecosystem came to be, and what it will take to sustain it. We heard stories of successful startups, failed ventures, corporate collaborations, the tides of investment funding, and how so many large pieces of the ecosystem have shifted into place alongside one another over the decades.

But one thing that each person continually reinforced was the power of relationships. Small interactions and anecdotes that started wonderful and unpredictable chains of events. A new acquaintance taking a big leap of faith and trust. Passionate but unfulfilled people deciding to take a risk and pursue their vision. Generosity. Humility. Collaboration.

If there were a core ethos of Chicago's innovation ecosystem, it would be: innovation is for everyone. Whatever your role is within your community, you can choose to take actions that push your organization, your neighborhood, and your city forward.

It can be an uphill battle at times, but it always is for those disrupting the status quo. And when those risk takers and disrupters break new ground, it lays a foundation for those who follow to find success as well. Shivani Vora, Managing Director of Accenture's Innovation Hub, explains, "Innovators embrace uncertainty and go where there is no path. Thus, they build the path for others." Anyone can be a champion for innovation. Anyone can be a connector. Anyone can recognize and celebrate risk takers. Anyone can be a risk taker themselves. Humans thrive on problem solving, creating, and experimenting. Everyone has an innovator within themselves, and every innovation ecosystem has a foundation of solution-minded, action-oriented people working together. A new ecosystem might start with a handful of passionate, values-driven individuals and grow in a lifetime to become a city with national prominence.

Your path to impact can start with understanding your own landscape. What are the need areas in your community? Where are new ideas coming from? What are the core, innate values of your region? Where can you find the resources to support problem solving and bring ideas to life? Do these resources even exist? How far do you have to go to find them; or will you need to create them as well?

Maybe there are events in your community that bring together innovators, technologists, and problem solvers. You're probably not alone; there are more than likely community leaders out there trying to pursue a vision for developing an innovation ecosystem as well. What can you learn about their activity? How can you help?

Or maybe you have a big idea of your own, one that you believe could really add value to people's lives. What would it look like to take that first step? Maybe it involves talking to someone with experience in the related industry. Maybe it involves taking a class, building a prototype, or talking to potential customers and investors about the need for your solution.

Innovation has often been displayed as a lonely effort, with images of the rogue entrepreneur trying to bootstrap their way to realizing their vision, or an antisocial engineer tirelessly building prototypes in his or her garage. But in reality, no one goes it alone. Like our young innovators Aanya and Florian at the beginning of this book, excited to show the world their ChargeAir invention, the path from idea to reality involves leapfrogging from connection to connection, resource to resource, and navigating the innovation ecosystem while discovering like-minded, passionate people along the way.

And if you find you have turned over every stone only to realize that your region's innovation ecosystem is nowhere to be found, will you build it?

INDEX

Index